PS 3565 .A8 W43 1994

Oates, Joyce Carol, 1938-

"Where are you going, where
have you been?"

"Where Are You Going, Where Have You Been?"

Women Writers
Texts and Contexts

SERIES EDITORS	SERIES BOARD
THOMAS L. ERSKINE *Salisbury State University*	MARTHA BANTA *University of California at Los Angeles*
CONNIE L. RICHARDS *Salisbury State University*	BARBARA T. CHRISTIAN *University of California at Berkeley*
	PAUL LAUTER *Trinity College*

VOLUMES IN THE SERIES

CHARLOTTE PERKINS GILMAN, "The Yellow Wallpaper"
Edited by Thomas L. Erskine and Connie L. Richards, Salisbury State University

JOYCE CAROL OATES, "Where Are You Going, Where Have You Been?"
Edited by Elaine Showalter, Princeton University

FLANNERY O'CONNOR, "A Good Man Is Hard to Find"
Edited by Frederick Asals, University of Toronto

TILLIE OLSEN, "Tell Me a Riddle"
Edited by Deborah Silverton Rosenfelt, University of Maryland, College Park

KATHERINE ANNE PORTER, "Flowering Judas"
Edited by Virginia Spencer Carr, Georgia State University

LESLIE MARMON SILKO, "Yellow Woman"
Edited by Melody Graulich, University of New Hampshire

ALICE WALKER, "Everyday Use"
Edited by Barbara T. Christian, University of California, Berkeley

HISAYE YAMAMOTO, "Seventeen Syllables"
Edited by King-Kok Cheung, University of California, Los Angeles

"Where Are You Going, Where Have You Been?"

JOYCE CAROL OATES ∎

Edited and with an introduction by
ELAINE SHOWALTER

Rutgers University Press
New Brunswick, New Jersey

4/96   #3031954+

Library of Congress Cataloging-in-Publication Data

Oates, Joyce Carol, 1938–
    "Where are you going, where have you been?" / Joyce Carol Oates ;
edited and with an introduction by Elaine Showalter.
    p.   cm. — (Women writers)
    Includes bibliographical references (p.)
    ISBN 0-8135-2134-3 (cloth) — ISBN 0-8135-2135-1 (pbk.)
    1. Teenage girls—United States—Fiction.   2. Serial murders—United
States—Fiction.   I. Showalter, Elaine.   II. Title.   III. Series: Women
writers (New Brunswick, N.J.)
    PS 3565.A8W43   1994
    813'.54—dc20   94-11284
                                                                            CIP

British Cataloging-in-Publication information available

❏ Contents ■

v

❏ Introduction

Introduction

Among the four hundred short stories that Joyce Carol Oates has published during her career, "Where Are You Going, Where Have You Been?" remains the best known, most anthologized, and most widely discussed. Inspired by a magazine story about a teenage killer in Arizona, it was first published in the literary magazine *Epoch* in fall 1966 and then selected for *The Best American Short Stories* (1967) and *The O. Henry Awards* (1968). In recent years, it has been reprinted as part of the feminist literary canon in *The Norton Anthology of Literature by Women* (1985), edited by Sandra Gilbert and Susan Gubar; and Oates has drawn attention to the centrality of the story in her literary development by using it as the overall title of two collections of her short stories: *Where Are You Going, Where Have You Been?: Stories of Young America* (1974) and *Where Are You Going, Where Have You Been?: Selected Early Stories* (1993). In 1986, the story was the basis of a commercially successful film, *Smooth Talk*, directed by Joyce Chopra, which in its turn became the subject of much feminist debate.

Following the changes from *Life* reporter Don Moser's account of "The Pied Piper of Tucson," to Oates's masterpiece, to the movie *Smooth Talk* gives us the opportunity to see how the literary imagination transforms raw material into art, and to understand these different genres and texts as related but autonomous works. Oates has described her many stories and novels as "tributaries flowing into a single river"; so it is not surprising that "Where Are You Going" should contain many elements that have been characteristic in her work, including the blurring of realism and the supernatural, and the effort to bear witness "for those who can't speak for themselves."[1] The story also takes up troubling subjects that have continued to occupy her in her fiction: the romantic longings and limited

3

options of adolescents, especially girls; the sexual victimization of women; the psychology of serial killers; and the American obsession with violence.

Oates has described the form of "Where Are You Going" as "psychological realism"; or "realistic allegory," a fictional mode that is "Hawthornean, romantic, shading into parable."[2] At the same time, the story deals with a terrifying possibility of contemporary American life, a situation of invasion, abduction, and probable rape and murder, which meets us in every morning's headlines and every evening's television news. For women who live with these fears, as the white women of Hawthorne's age did not, the formal and abstract elements of "Where Are You Going" will be measured against its indictment of an American social disorder.

Joyce Carol Oates is among the most distinguished writers of her generation, but the success story of an American woman writer is always different from the normative success story designed for men. We have no expectations of the great American woman novelist, no myths of her growing up, or coming of age. "I don't have any long list of things like busboy, Western Union boy, short-order cook, naval officer—all of those things are on most people's dust jackets," Oates has commented about her relatively uneventful life.[3] While her career more closely resembles the pattern of early creativity, literary immersion, and intellectual omniverousness established by American women writers like Margaret Fuller and Edith Wharton, she has written more, in a variety of genres, than any comparable American writer of this century.

Born on June 16, 1938, in rural Lockport, New York, Oates grew up in a working-class Catholic family and attended a one-room schoolhouse, where her teacher, Mrs. Dietz, taught eight grades. "For decades," she writes, "my memory of my first teacher was that of a childs'-eye view of a giantess, or a deity: could Mrs. Dietz really have been as tall as I remembered?"[4] As a schoolchild, she read the American classics in a tattered copy of the *Treasure of American Literature:* Franklin, Irving, Hawthorne, Melville, Emerson, Thoreau, Poe, and Twain. Few women writers were included among these first literary Gods, for in the process of national canonization, American women writers and artists such as Harriet Beecher

4

Stowe or Kate Chopin had been left out of anthologies. Later, in her teens, she read Emily Dickinson and the Brontës, and still later, Flannery O'Connor.

Although their own education had been cut short by the Depression, her parents, Frederic and Carolina Oates, were both devoted readers who supported their daughter's emerging intellectual and literary gifts. She was given a typewriter by her grandmother when she was fourteen, and began to train herself "by writing novel after novel."[5] When she was fifteen, she submitted her first novel to a publisher; it was rejected as too depressing for young readers.[6] But Oates won all the school prizes, including a New York State Regents Scholarship to Syracuse University. There she devoured philosophy and literature, especially Nietzsche, Kafka, and Faulkner, and graduated class valedictorian, *summa cum laude*, and Phi Beta Kappa in 1960. During her junior year at Syracuse her short story "In the Old World" won the *Mademoiselle* fiction award. "We never really thought she'd be *this* successful," her father remarks. "It all started when she was in college and won that fiction contest at *Mademoiselle*. Everything just took off from there."[7]

At this stage of her life, Oates was planning to become an English professor; she entered graduate school at the University of Wisconsin, where she met and married another student, Raymond Smith. She was beginning her doctoral work at Rice University when one of her stories was selected for the honor roll of *Best American Short Stories*, and she gave up academic criticism for fiction, although she has continued to teach throughout her career. In 1962, Oates and Smith moved to Detroit, and she was deeply marked by the racial violence that finally exploded in the riots of 1967. "Moving to Detroit in the early 1960s changed my life completely," she has said. "I would have been a writer . . . but living in Detroit, enduring the extraordinary racial tensions of that city . . . made me want to write directly about the serious social concerns of our time."[8] Her novel *them*, which reflects the apocalyptic sensibility of the period, received the National Book Award in 1970. From 1967 to 1978, Oates and Smith taught at the University of Windsor in Canada, a decade in which she published twenty-seven books—short stories, novels, poetry, plays, and criticism. "I have a laughably Balzacian ambition to get the whole world into a book," she told an interviewer in 1972.[9]

In 1978, Oates joined the faculty of Princeton University where she is now Roger Berlind Professor of the Humanities. Like Virginia and Leonard Woolf, Oates and Smith are a literary team who have established a journal, *The Ontario Review*, and a publishing company, The Ontario Review Press. Having their own press gives them the power to sponsor other writers, artists, and translators as well as to publish some of Oates's own work. Oates also writes fiction under the pseudonym "Rosamond Smith." The move to Princeton inaugurated a new, more public phase of her career. She has travelled extensively in the United States and Europe, and her writing continues to reflect an enormous range of interests in contemporary American life, from boxing to politics. "For a serious American writer—especially for a woman writer," Oates told an interviewer in 1992, "This is by far the best era in which to live."[10]

The huge ambition, formidable intelligence, and vast range of Oates's work has nonetheless unsettled the stereotypes of those critics who still equate greatness with masculinity. From early in her career, Oates has often been judged in terms of the gender-determined norms of American literature, criticized for her enormous literary productivity and for the violence of her drama and fiction. She has always scorned such criticism as sexist. "If the lot of womankind has not yet widely diverged from that romantically envisioned by our Moral Majority," Oates wrote in 1981, ". . . the lot of the woman writer has been just as severely circumscribed. War, rape, murder and the more colorful minor crimes evidently fall within the exclusive province of male action."[11] In the 1980s and 1990s, her work has moved toward more explicitly feminist themes.

Yet Oates has also been reluctant to describe herself as a "woman writer" or a "feminist writer." Instead, she calls herself a "(woman) writer," an artist whose imagination and ambition is genderless, yet who knows her social identity constrained by cultural expectations and by the literary traditions of sexual difference. Her thinking on the "ontological status of the writer who is also a woman' is deeply sympathetic to feminist concerns but firm in its distinctions between the serious writer's genderless imagination, and the sexually-specific reception and critical understanding of her work. "A woman who writes is a writer by her own definition," she has observed, "but she is a *woman* writer by others' definitions."[12]

"Where Are You Going" reflects many of the ideas and attitudes of the 1960s, but is set in a teenage culture more like the 1950s. Such recognizable details of American adolescent life as popular music, radio disc jockeys, cars, drive-in restaurants, and shopping plazas feature in the plot, yet they also seem fixed in an unreal and stylized teenage past shaped by movies, before mall rats, drugs, date rape, or The Pill. Connie's fantasy world is the world of James Dean, Natalie Wood, and *Rebel Without a Cause*. Her coming-of-age story also anticipates the coming-of-age of American society, its emergence from the hazy dreams and social innocence of the 1950s into the harsher realities of random violence, war, and crime. Oates has located the story in the "transformational years" of the 1960s, when she saw "a new morality . . . emerging in America," a morality "intuitively understood" by her younger readers who could see in it not "morbidity, absurdity, and a sense that life is meaningless," but rather the portrayal of "human beings struggling heroically to define personal identity in the face of death itself."[13]

In an early essay, Oates noted that she often wrote stories based on newspaper headlines: "It is the very skeletal nature of the newspaper, I think, that attracts me to it, the need it inspires in me to give flesh to such neatly and thinly-told tales."[14] The skeleton of "Where Are You Going" was the saga of an American teenage murderer, Charles Schmid, which was written up in *Life* magazine, as well as other news magazines, during the winter of 1965–1966. Oates has commented that she deliberately did not read the *Life* article all the way through, in order not "to be distracted by too much detail," but that it captured her interest: "There have always been psychopathic killers, serial murderers, and interest in them; as how could there fail to be, given our human predilection for horror, 'the fascination of the abomination' . . . . For the writer, the serial killer is, abstractly, an analogue of the imagination's caprices and amorality; the sense that, no matter the dictates and even the wishes of the conscious, social self, the life or will or purpose of the imagination is incomprehensible, unpredictable."[15]

Charles Schmid was a twenty-three-year-old ex-high school student who had been suspended in his senior year for stealing tools from a welding class. He had taken to hanging out by the high school, picking up girls for rides in his gold convertible. Ultimately he murdered three of them, while other teenagers served as accomplices. In March 1966 Schmid was convicted of murder and sentenced to die in the Arizona gas chamber, but he was killed by another inmate before the sentence could be carried out.[16]

Schmid's story attracted a great deal of attention during a period when teenage runaways, the evils of rock and roll, and adolescent sexuality were much debated in the news, and before the American public had become numbed by stories of serial killers. Readers were fascinated by the way Schmid had modelled himself on his idol, Elvis Presley, and by his self-dramatizing lies. But the teenage girls he entranced and murdered are much less colorful characters in the news stories. Such girls were the other side of the American fantasies of the early 1960s—the Barbie dolls, Gidgets, and groupies of the years just before the women's movement. Oates, however, turned the familiar story of the serial killer inside-out by taking the victim as her protagonist, and by taking her seriously. Her sense of what is tragic in Connie's "trashy dreams," and what is heroic in her fate, is typical of her compassion for the women often rendered silent and inarticulate in American society.

In 1970, Oates included "Where Are You Going" in her third collection of short stories, *The Wheel of Love*. While her earlier collections had included all her published short fiction, with *The Wheel of Love* she began to select and shape her books of stories around a theme, so that they were "not assemblages of disparate material but wholes with unifying strategies of organization."[17] The unifying theme of *The Wheel of Love,* she told an interviewer in 1970, was "different forms of love, mainly in family relationships"; she had originally planned to call the book *Love Stories*.[18] Other stories in the collection included the prize-winning "In the Region of Ice,"

"The Wheel of Love," and "How I Contemplated the World from the Detroit House of Correction and Began My Life Over Again."

Oates has written and commented on "Where Are You Going" in numerous interviews and essays in the decades since its publication. She has explained that the story came to her "more or less in a piece" after hearing Bob Dylan's song "It's All Over Now, Baby Blue" and then reading about a killer in the Southwest and thinking about "the old legends and folk songs of Death and the Maiden."[19] She dedicated the original story to Dylan because the "hauntingly elegiac" song seemed appropriate "to the dreamy, yet highly charged atmosphere of Connie's world"; in recent versions she has omitted this dedication as being dated, but it is part of the critical history of the story.[20] As she notes in the essay in this book, she first imagined Connie as both a realistic American teenager of her time and place, and the doomed "maiden" of legend. Initially she saw the story as "an allegory of the fatal attractions of death. . . . An innocent young girl . . . mistakes death for erotic romance of a particularly American/trashy sort." But as the story developed, she became more interested in its "moments of grace"—the "dramatic turn of action" at the end, "when the presumably doomed Connie makes a decision to accept her fate with dignity and to spare her family's involvement in this fate."[21] "At the end of the story," she has commented, "Connie transcends her Connie-self—her merely local, teenage, American self. So, confronted with death, we are obliged to be equal to it. Or to try. To merely sexualize the story trivializes it."[22]

In the 1960s and 1970s, "Where Are You Going" was most frequently read by critics as an allegory of good and evil, with Arnold Friend as a satanic figure. Many critics took the mother's point of view, condemning Connie's "trashy values," and boy-craziness, and blaming the debased adolescent culture of her world for her susceptibility to the fatal seduction. Critics analyzed the story's use of popular music, compared Arnold Friend to Bob Dylan and Ellie Oscar to Elvis Presley, and tried to decipher the numbers on Arnold's car. They were shocked by the ending of the story, but did not see Connie's yearnings as meaningful or view her final act as courageous.

Only very recently has Oates been discussed as a feminist writer. Indeed, in 1970, a reviewer of *The Wheel of Love* insisted that the characters "have no connection with the movement for women's liberation."[23] Feminist critics who wrote about Oates in the 1970s emphasized her negative images of women, rather than the feminist consciousness behind the work. Greg Johnson, a critic who is also writing a biography of Oates, is among those who take the opposite view. He argues that "Where Are You Going?" is among the earliest of Oates's stories to show "explicitly feminist concerns." Indeed, according to Johnson, the story is a "feminist allegory" in which Connie is "surrendering her autonomous selfhood to male desire and domination. Her characterization as a typical girl reaching sexual maturity suggests that her fate represents that suffered by most young women—unwillingly and in secret terror—even in America in the 1960s." Overall, he concludes, "Where Are You Going?" is "a cautionary tale, suggesting that young women are actually 'going' exactly where their mothers and grandmothers have already 'been'"—into sexual bondage at the hands of a male "Friend."[24]

The issues of feminist allegory became more evident in 1986, when "Where Are You Going, Where Have You Been?" was made into a movie called *Smooth Talk,* with a screenplay by Tom Cole and direction by Joyce Chopra, who had made her reputation as a feminist director of documentary films including *Girls at Twelve* and *Joyce at 34. Smooth Talk* starred Laura Dern as Connie, Treat Williams as Arnold Friend, and Mary Kay Place as Connie's mother, with songs by James Taylor. In a dark irony that strikes at the very heart of the story, the film was shot in Petaluma, California, then imagined as a model of safe, small-town America, but in 1993 the place where twelve-year-old Polly Klass was abducted and murdered by a psychopath who broke into her house. In adapting the story for the screen, Cole and Chopra made a number of changes in the plot, developing the roles of Connie's girlfriends and family. Most important, they revised the ending, so that after driving away with Arnold in his convertible, Connie returns to her home. She tells Arnold firmly that she does not want to see him again, and then seems softened and reconciled to her family.

The success of the film sent reviewers back to the story, and occasioned an intense debate over the feminist implications and contemporary relevance of both story and movie. To many critics, the story was shockingly anti-feminist in its mobilization of women's fears about sexuality. Writing in the film journal *Cinéaste*, for example, Elayne Rapping described the story as a Cinderella tale in reverse, where the "wicked stepmothers and ugly stepsisters get their revenge on the 'popular' one, the one who "thinks she's so pretty.'" In Rapping's view, both film and story were "preoccupied with sexual danger and fear, with the menacing image of men as ruthless, semideranged predators," and despite its ending, the film "resurrects a puritanical fear of female sexuality and the old good girl/bad girl dichotomy which uses that fear to keep women sexually repressed and at war with each other."[25]

A major difference between the story and the movie was the intense degree of identification viewers, particularly women viewers, felt with Connie. Whether they were teenage girls or middle-aged mothers, ordinary filmgoers or experienced film critics, women viewers had strong reactions to Connie's behavior. Audiences used to Hollywood horror films about stalkers and slashers, and to everyday fears of sexual violence, were disturbed by Connie's recklessness, and frightened by her encounter with Arnold Friend, and thus the film's effort to incorporate both the realistic and the symbolic elements of the story ran into serious difficulties. As Andrew Sarris pointed out, this could partly be explained by the difference in genres: "The tendency of readers of fiction is to identify with the sensibility of the writer and to discern that sensibility through the transparency of the literary characters. Moviegoers identify more with the corporeal identity of the actors and actresses on the screen, and associate their own destinies and fantasies with the idealized figures on the mobile and luminous canvas."[26]

Oates has always made clear that "*Smooth Talk*, with its different title, is an autonomous work."[27] In an essay originally written for the *New York Times* and reprinted in this volume, she discussed her own reactions to the film, emphasizing the historical and generic differences between her ending and the one chosen by Joyce Chopra. Whereas "Where Are

11

You Going, Where Have You Been?" "defines itself as allegorical in its conclusion," the film makes Connie a "'typical' teenaged girl" of today, whose "loss of virginity is bittersweet but not necessarily tragic." The resonances of Oates's ending, with its allusions to "the vast sunlit reaches of the land" to which Connie is going, suggests an awakening that is "impossible to transfigure into film."

The critical essays and reviews in this volume provide a cross-section of the most stimulating responses both to the story and the film. They represent different phases in the critical reception of Oates's work, and in the interpretation of her psychological realism. No case book on Oates's fiction, however, can supply a full set of answers to all the disturbing questions the story will raise for a reader. As Oates has warned, "Every person dreams, and every dreamer is a kind of artist. The formal artist is one who arranges his dreams into a shape that can be experienced by other people. There is no guarantee that art will be understood, not even by the artist; it is not meant to be understood but to be experienced."[28]

The first two essays illuminate the differences between social and metaphorical interpretations of the story. Is it reality or dream? At one extreme, Marie Urbanski's essay describes the story as an "existential allegory," in which the author's realistic "trappings" should not obscure her allegorical design of "Everyman's transition from the illusion of free will to the realization of externally determined fate." On the other side, in opposition to Urbanski and other critics who see the story as a fable, Tom Quirk announces his discovery of Oates's source: the case of Charles Schmid. In his 1981 essay, he shows how many of the details of the story were indebted to details of news reports of the Pied Piper of Tucson, and insists that the people, events, and evil Oates portrayed in her story were all too real. In Quirk's view, the story is not a timeless allegory of existential fate, but a specific critique of the "antique values" of the American Dream.

Yet, as Quirk also acknowledges, Oates is an artist rather than a journalist, and her fiction is an imaginative transformation of the actual into something new and strange. Thus other critics have emphasized the story's literary and mythic elements. In "The Stranger Within," Joan Winslow notes the parallels between Oates and Hawthorne's "Young Goodman Brown" as stories of sexual initiation and repression. Winslow focuses on the passage which describes the two sides of Connie's personality, "one for home and one for anywhere that was not home," and sees Connie's encounter with Arnold Friend as a meeting with a devil figure who is really the demonic side of herself. In both Hawthorne and Oates, the story can be read as a dream and "as a psychological analysis of the emotional state which could create such a dream."

Joyce W. Wegs's essay focuses on Oates's use of the grotesque to show the terror and mystery behind everyday reality. In her reading, Connie's "grotesquely false values" derived from romance and popular culture substitute for a deeper morality or spirituality; and her family and society are equally devoid of religious content. Arnold Friend is a satanic figure, "the incarnation of Connie's unconscious erotic desires and dreams, but in uncontrollable nightmare form." Picking up on suggestions by Winslow and Wegs, Larry Rubin argues that the Arnold Friend episode is actually Connie's dream, a quasi-rape fantasy that she falls into when she is alone at home drying her hair. In Rubin's view, Oates is portraying Connie's "compulsive sex drive" as a destructive force which will ruin her not only physically but also morally. For the "uninitiated female," a "deep-rooted desire for ultimate sexual gratification" may be profoundly dangerous.

In contrast to essays which see Connie's fate as the result of her trashy teenage dreams or her dangerous sexuality and blame the vapidity of her society for her false values, Gretchen Schulz and R.J.R. Rockwood locate the story in a tradition of cautionary narratives and folklore about women's identity and behavior, interpreting Connie's behavior from a psychoanalytic perspective. They direct our attention to motifs from the many fairy tales—the Pied Piper, Snow White, Cinderella, Sleeping Beauty, Rapunzel, Little Red Riding Hood, and the Three Little Pigs—woven into Oates's story. Following the work of Bruno Bettelheim, they argue that these fairy tales are symbolic maps of female adolescent conflict, and that Connie is a troubled adolescent struggling with "unresolved oedipal conflict, aggravated by sibling rivalry" and unable to integrate her unconscious and conscious desires. Schulz and

Rockwood regard the encounter with Arnold Friend as both another fairy tale and a case study of Connie's lapse into psychosis, "a terrifying schizophrenic separation from reality, with prognosis for recovery extremely poor."

Christina M. Gillis acknowledges the importance of fairy tales, fantasies, and dreams in "Where Are You Going," but also stresses women's vulnerability to seduction and rape, both in the real world and in the traditions of fiction, where the interior spaces of the female body and of the home emphasize issues of threshold, invasion, privacy, and attack. Gillis places responsibility for the story's outcome on Arnold Friend, the invader who does not respect the spatial limits of Connie's world and who finally uses threats against her family to force her out. In Gillis's reading, Connie's age and gender, not her values or desires, make her a vulnerable victim.

The essays by B. Ruby Rich and Brenda O. Daly provide different viewpoints on the film adaptation, *Smooth Talk*. Writing in *The Village Voice,* Rich protests the movie's seeming endorsement of a retrograde message: sex is dangerous for teenage girls. Connie is punished for her flirtatiousness, her sexuality, her sense of adventure: "She was asking for it, wasn't she? Just looking for it, right? We're back in the familiar terrain of Blame the Victim Land." But while Daly agrees that Chopra uses the camera and the soundtrack to "enforce a sexual/spatial system of inequalities," she also argues that the movie is not a typical Hollywood horror film which exploits female sexual vulnerability. In the film, Connie survives; the evolution of her consciousness, which was the subject of Oates's story, is transformed into assertiveness and will. Her story is one of "joy in her awakening sexuality" and rebellion against the conventional morality of her mother and sister. While Oates's ending is metaphysical, involving self-knowledge in the face of darkness, Chopra's ending is more material, involving Connie's triumph over the invader. "The difference between Oates's Connie and Chopra's Connie," Daly concludes, "is but one instance of our cultural metamorphosis during the past 20–25 years."

For the fullest understanding of "Where Are You Going," one which takes Connie seriously, we need to consider its place in a tradition of women's writing, as well as within the classic male tradition most critics have examined as influences or parallels. The title "Where Are You Going, Where Have You Been?" first strikes us as the parent's nagging question to the child. Yet it is also a metaphysical question about Connie's life, and about the experience and destiny of women. Oates invokes both concrete detail and literary mythology to emphasize the double story of adolescent coming-of-age and female sexual vulnerability.

One important myth is the story of Demeter and Persephone, which has been paradigmatic for American women writers at least since the nineteenth century.[29] In the classical version of the myth, as told in Ovid's *Metamorphoses*, the young Persephone is gathering flowers in a field when she is surprised by Hades, who carries her away in his chariot to the underworld. There she grows hungry and eats the seeds of a pomegranate. Because she has consumed the seeds, her mother Demeter cannot bring her back to earth, but must accept the gods' proposal that Persephone should spend half the year in the realm of the dead with Hades and only half on earth with her. As the story has been interpreted by American women writers, however, it becomes a parable of the woman artist's rite of passage, her necessary separation from the mother's world of reproductive sexuality and nurturance to the dark underworld of passion, creativity, and independence.[30] As Oates has commented with regard to her novel *American Appetites*, the daughter "has to define herself in terms of the mother and she has to define herself in opposition to the mother, in order to have any identity. . . . Many daughters are close to [and] love their mothers enormously, but the love is so strong it has to be denied if they are to be two people."[31]

The myth of Demeter and Persephone can also be described in Freudian terms, as the daughter's necessary individuation and transfer of attachment from the mother to the father. But this process is fraught with internal and external violence. As Marilyn Wesley has explained, the dangers of the transition are "often expressed in stories of imminent rape," as the daughter finds "not liberation from the mother's values, but the overwhelming evidence of her powerlessness within the patriarchal system." Wesley has traced a three-stage process of the American daughter's individuation in

15

Oates's fiction: First, the necessity of differentiating a self separate from the mother; second, the consciousness of rape as a cultural condition that implies the victimization of the female; and third, the attempt to counter the threat of violence through the discovery of forms of perception such as art, literature, or education that may balance order and vitality. She sees this pattern in "Where Are You Going," especially in the ending. Although Arnold Friend is a psychopath, his function in the story is also to force Connie into recognizing the limiting codes of the family. He is a transgressive figure "of limit and challenge" who appears in various guises throughout Oates's work.[32]

In "Where Are You Going," Connie is eager to separate from the dull domestic world of her mother and sister, but also plays out a charade of conflict with her mother that masks an uneasy intimacy and identity. Connie fears that life is taking her to a moment in which she too will be scuffling around in old bedroom slippers with nothing but photos to remind her of her adolescent flowering, nothing but a tired, silent husband to remind her of the sweet caresses of love. In the pre-feminist milieu of the story, sisterhood is no more powerful than motherhood. Bonds between women are weak and superficial. Connie and her sister June seem to have nothing in common; Connie's girlfriends are scarcely important enough to be named. When they go out together, it is not to be together but to escape from their parents and to find boys. In the world of the story, women cannot group together for mutual support, but only gang up against a third, as Connie's mother shows when she "complained over the telephone to one sister about the other, then the other called up and the two of them complained about the third one."

Connie's past and future, the place where she has been and where she is going, is symbolized by her mother's body and her mother's house. Her abduction from this claustrophobic world at the hands of Arnold Friend is both terrifying and liberatory. "Where Are You Going" shares many characteristics of the fictional genre of the Female Gothic, a classic form of feminine narrative from the eighteenth century to the present, which deals with female sexuality, maternity, and creativity. In its original form, established by novels like Anne

Radcliffe's *The Mysteries of Udolpho,* a young heroine is kidnapped by masked bandits and taken to a haunted castle or ruined abbey, where she is threatened by an older, dark, powerful man, who may turn out to be her lover or her father. (Oates has commented in the essay on the film reprinted here that she wished that she had "built up the father, suggesting, as subtly as I could, an attraction there paralleling the attraction Connie feels for her seducer, Arnold Friend.") Often the heroine's mother is also a prisoner in the castle or has died there and indeed the castle or enclosed space is another symbol of the maternal body. In bravely confronting these spectral images in her family romance, the heroine comes to terms with her own identity and destiny.

The Gothic heroine is kidnapped in part because conventions of femininity make it otherwise almost impossible for her to move. Connie, too, is virtually immobilized by her sex and her age. At fifteen, she is too young to drive a car, but in any case, in the story only boys and men seem to drive. If the girls want to go to the movies, they have to find a father to drive them; if they want sexual privacy with a boy, his car provides it. Connie is always at the mercy of men who will come with a vehicle to take her away, to take her somewhere else. Women have no agency, no vehicle, no wheels. It's not coincidental that Arnold Friend's golden convertible is part of his magic.

Moreover, like Austen's Catherine Norland in *Northanger Abbey,* Connie's "trashy daydreams" are shaped by popular culture, and she sees her little world through the rosy lens of romantic films. The drive-in restaurant is a "sacred building" and Connie does not imagine anything bigger or better in the city. The shopping plaza and the moviehouse are enough for her; and adolescent sex has been just "the way it was in movies and promised in songs." But whatever the promises of songs, the story gives Connie few real choices for the future. She can be a working drudge like her sister, or a housewife drudge like her mother. Connie's father, the man inside the house—it is, according to Arnold Friend, her "daddy's house"— also models a future. His role in Connie's fantasies and her real life is negligible, though he plays a subtle role as a potential liberator and object of desire. Only a hazy eroticism, a

17

combination of the sun, the music, and youth, gives Connie joy; but in the Gothic tradition she inhabits, such violent delights have violent ends.

Yet we need to remember that allegories also have a history, and belong to historical moments. Oates's Connie both transcends the moment of her creation and belongs to it, just as Chopra's Connie reflects the assumptions and values of 1986. Returning to the story of teen-age girls in 1993, Oates wrote *Foxfire: Confessions of a Girl Gang,* in which another group of girls in the late 1950s get hold of their own car and fight back against the sexual violence of men. Although Connie's efforts to define her own identity take her into a nightmare world where sexual initiation and female desire have fatal consequences, "Where Are You Going, Where Have You Been?" is a classic which confronts us unforgettably with the power and freedom of the imagination.

☐ *Notes* ∎

1. Joyce Carol Oates, "Afterword," *Where Are You Going, Where Have You Been?* (Princeton: Ontario Review Press, 1993), 519, 521.

2. Joyce Carol Oates, "Preface," *Stories of Young America* (Greenwich, Connecticut: Fawcett, 1974), 10; "'Where Are You Going, Where Have You Been?' and *Smooth Talk:* Short Story into Film," reprinted here.

3. Linda Kuehl, "An Interview with Joyce Carol Oates," *Commonweal* (December 5, 1969), in Lee Milazzo, ed., *Conversations with Joyce Carol Oates* (Jackson: University Press of Mississippi, 1989), 13.

4. Joyce Carol Oates, "Introduction," *The Best American Essays 1991* (New York: Ticknor & Fields, 1991), xiv.

5. Robert Phillips, "Joyce Carol Oates; The Art of Fiction LXXII," *Paris Review* (Fall 1978), in *Conversations,* 76.

6. Frank McLaughlin, "A Conversation with Joyce Carol Oates," from *Writing!* (September 1985), in *Conversations,* 123.

7. Quoted in Jay Parini, "My Writing is Full of Lives I Might Have Led," *Boston Globe Magazine* (August 2, 1987), 64.

8. McLaughlin, "A Conversation," in *Conversations,* 125.

9. Walter Clemons, "Joyce Carol Oates: Love and Violence," *Newsweek* (December 11, 1972), in *Conversations*, 33.

10. Interview with Elaine Showalter.

11. Joyce Carol Oates, "Why Is Your Writing So Violent?," *The New York Times Book Review* (March 25, 1981), 35.

12. Joyce Carol Oates, "(Woman) Writer: Theory and Practice," in *(Woman) Writer: Occasions and Opportunities* (New York: Dutton, 1988), 27–28.

13. "Preface," *Stories of Young America*.

14. Joyce Carol Oates, "The Nature of Short Fiction; or, The Nature of My Short Fiction," in Frank A. Dickson and Sandra Smythe, *Handbook of Short Story Writing* (Writers Digest: Cincinnati), xiv.

15. Interview with Elaine Showalter.

16. See "Growing Up in Tucson," *Time* (March 11, 1966), 28.

17. "Afterword," *Where Are You Going*, 521.

18. Kuehl, "An Interview," in *Conversations*, 12, 13.

19. "Interview with Joyce Carol Oates," in John R. Knott, Jr., and Christopher R. Keaske, eds., *Mirrors: An Introduction to Literature*, 2nd ed. (San Francisco: Canfield Press, 1975), 18–19.

20. Interview with Elaine Showalter.

21. "Afterword," *Where Are You Going*, 522.

22. Interview with Elaine Showalter.

23. Charles L. Markmann, "The Terror of Love," *Nation* 14 (December 1970), 636.

24. Johnson, *Understanding Joyce Carol Oates* (Columbia: University of South Carolina Press, 1987), 95, 103.

25. Elayne Rapping, "Smooth Talk," *Cineaste* 15 (1986), 36–37.

26. Andrew Sarris, "Teenage Gothic," *Village Voice* (March 4, 1986), 53.

27. Interview with Elaine Showalter.

28. Joyce Carol Oates, "Fictions, Dreams, Revelations," in *Scenes from American Life: Contemporary Short Fiction* (New York: Random House, 1973), vii–viii.

29. See Josephine Donovan, *After the Fall: The Demeter–Persephone Myth in Wharton, Cather, and Glasgow* (University Park: Pennsylvania State University Press, 1989).

30. For an excellent account of one writer's use of the myth,

see Candace Waid, *Edith Wharton's Letters from the Underworld* (Chapel Hill: University of North Carolina Press), 1990.

31. "Joyce Carol Oates" in *Inter/View,* ed. Mickey Pearlman and Katherine Usher Henderson (Lexington: The University Press of Kentucky, 1990), 44.

32. Marilyn C. Wesley, *Refusal and Transgression in Joyce Carol Oates' Fiction* (Westport, Connecticut: Greenwood Press, 1993), 127–28, 44, 145–46.

Thanks to Madere Olivar and Wendy Chun for research assistance on this volume.

—E. S.

❑ Chronology ■

1938 Born on June 16 to Carolina and Frederic Oates, the eldest of three children. Grows up on her maternal grandparents' farm in Erie County, outside Lockport, New York.

1956 Enters Syracuse University on New York State Regents scholarship.

1959 Co-winner, first prize, *Mademoiselle* College Fiction Contest for "In the Old World" (story).

1960 Graduates, class valedictorian and Phi Beta Kappa; B.A. in English, minor in philosophy. Enters graduate English program at University of Wisconsin, Madison, on fellowship; meets Raymond Joseph Smith, Jr.

1961 Marries Smith on January 23. Earns M.A., and enrolls in doctoral program at Rice University.

1962 Decides to become a writer after learning that one of her short stories was selected for the Honor Roll in Martha Foley's annual *Best American Short Stories* (1961).

1962 Teaches English Literature at University of Detroit until 1967. *By the North Gate* (first collection of short stories) is published.

1964 *With Shuddering Fall* (first novel) is published.

1965 "The Sweet Enemy" (play) premieres in New York City at Actor's Playhouse.

1966 "Where Are You Going, Where Have You Been?" first published in *Epoch*, Fall 1966.

1967 Joins Department of English Literature at University of Windsor, Canada, as Assistant Professor. Receives Guggenheim Fellowship, and O. Henry Prize Award, first prize, for "In the Region of Ice."

1968 Receives Rosenthal Foundation Award of the National Institute of Arts and Letters for *A Garden of Earthly Delights* (novel) and a National Endowment for the Humanities Grant. "Where Are You Going, Where Have You Been?" included in *Prize Stories: The O. Henry Awards 1968.*

1969 Wins Emily Clark Balch Short Story Competition, first prize, for "Convalescing" and second prize, O. Henry Prize Awards, for "Accomplished Desires."

1970 *them* (novel) receives National Book Award. Receives Special Award for continuing achievement, O. Henry Prize Awards and again in 1986.

1974 Begins publishing *Ontario Review: A North American Journal of the Arts* with husband.

1978 Elected member of American Academy and Institute of Arts and Letters. Becomes writer-in-residence and professor of English at Princeton University. Attends Soviet–American Writers Conference in New York City.

1980 Travels to Europe and parts of Eastern Europe.

1986 *Smooth Talk,* Joyce Chopra's film adaptation of "Where Are You Going, Where Have You Been?" is released.

1987 Appointed Roger S. Berlind Distinguished Professor in the Humanities at Princeton University.

1988 Receives St. Louis Literary Award.

1990 Receives Alan Swallow Award and Rea Award for the Short Story for "The Assignation."

1993 Publishes *Foxfire: Confessions of a Girl Gang.*

❑ Where Are You Going, Where Have You Been?

☐ Where Are You Going, Where Have You Been?

For Bob Dylan

Her name was Connie. She was fifteen and she
had a quick, nervous giggling habit of craning her neck
to glance into mirrors or checking other people's faces
to make sure her own was all right. Her mother, who noticed everything and knew everything and who hadn't
much reason any longer to look at her own face, always
scolded Connie about it. "Stop gawking at yourself. Who
are you? You think you're so pretty?" she would say.
Connie would raise her eyebrows at these familiar old
complaints and look right through her mother, into a
shadowy vision of herself as she was right at that moment: she knew she was pretty and that was everything. Her mother had been pretty once too, if you
could believe those old snapshots in the album, but now
her looks were gone and that was why she was always
after Connie.

"Why don't you keep your room clean like your
sister? How've you got your hair fixed—what the hell

stinks? Hair spray? You don't see your sister using that junk."

Her sister June was twenty-four and still lived at home. She was a secretary in the high school Connie attended, and if that wasn't bad enough—with her in the same building—she was so plain and chunky and steady that Connie had to hear her praised all the time by her mother and her mother's sisters. June did this, June did that, she saved money and helped clean the house and cooked and Connie couldn't do a thing, her mind was all filled with trashy daydreams. Their father was away at work most of the time and when he came home he wanted supper and he read the newspaper at supper and after supper he went to bed. He didn't bother talking much to them, but around his bent head Connie's mother kept picking at her until Connie wished her mother was dead and she herself was dead and it was all over. "She makes me want to throw up sometimes," she complained to her friends. She had a high, breathless, amused voice that made everything she said sound a little forced, whether it was sincere or not.

There was one good thing: June went places with girl friends of hers, girls who were just as plain and steady as she, and so when Connie wanted to do that her mother had no objections. The father of Connie's best girl friend drove the girls the three miles to town and left them at a shopping plaza so they could walk through the stores or go to a movie, and when he came to pick them up again at eleven he never bothered to ask what they had done.

They must have been familiar sights, walking around the shopping plaza in their shorts and flat ballerina slippers that always scuffed the sidewalk, with

charm bracelets jingling on their thin wrists; they
would lean together to whisper and laugh secretly if
someone passed who amused or interested them. Connie had long dark blond hair that drew anyone's eye to
it, and she wore part of it pulled up on her head and
puffed out and the rest of it she let fall down her back.
She wore a pullover jersey blouse that looked one way
when she was at home and another way when she was
away from home. Everything about her had two sides
to it, one for home and one for anywhere that was not
home: her walk, which could be childlike and bobbing,
or languid enough to make anyone think she was hearing music in her head; her mouth, which was pale and
smirking most of the time, but bright and pink on these
evenings out; her laugh, which was cynical and drawl-
ing at home—"Ha, ha, very funny"—but high-pitched
and nervous anywhere else, like the jingling of the
charms on her bracelet.

    Sometimes they did go shopping or to a movie,
but sometimes they went across the highway, ducking
fast across the busy road, to a drive-in restaurant where
older kids hung out. The restaurant was shaped like a
big bottle, though squatter than a real bottle, and on its
cap was a revolving figure of a grinning boy holding a
hamburger aloft. One night in midsummer they ran
across, breathless with daring, and right away someone
leaned out a car window and invited them over, but it
was just a boy from high school they didn't like. It made
them feel good to be able to ignore him. They went up
through the maze of parked and cruising cars to the
bright-lit, fly-infested restaurant, their faces pleased
and expectant as if they were entering a sacred building that loomed up out of the night to give them what
haven and blessing they yearned for. They sat at the

counter and crossed their legs at the ankles, their thin
shoulders rigid with excitement, and listened to the
music that made everything so good: the music was always in the background, like music at a church service;
it was something to depend upon.

A boy named Eddie came in to talk with them.
He sat backwards on his stool, turning himself jerkily
around in semicircles and then stopping and turning
back again, and after a while he asked Connie if she
would like something to eat. She said she would and so
she tapped her friend's arm on her way out—her friend
pulled her face up into a brave, droll look—and Connie
said she would meet her at eleven, across the way. "I
just hate to leave her like that," Connie said earnestly,
but the boy said that she wouldn't be alone for long.
So they went out to his car, and on the way Connie
couldn't help but let her eyes wander over the wind-
shields and faces all around her, her face gleaming with
a joy that had nothing to do with Eddie or even this
place; it might have been the music. She drew her
shoulders up and sucked in her breath with the pure
pleasure of being alive, and just at that moment she
happened to glance at a face just a few feet from hers.
It was a boy with shaggy black hair, in a convertible jalopy painted gold. He stared at her and then his lips
widened into a grin. Connie slit her eyes at him and
turned away, but she couldn't help glancing back and
there he was, still watching her. He wagged a finger
and laughed and said, "Gonna get you, baby," and Connie turned away again without Eddie noticing anything.

She spent three hours with him, at the restaurant
where they ate hamburgers and drank Cokes in wax
cups that were always sweating, and then down an alley a mile or so away, and when he left her off at five to

eleven only the movie house was still open at the plaza.
Her girl friend was there, talking with a boy. When
Connie came up, the two girls smiled at each other and
Connie said, "How was the movie?" and the girl said,
"*You* should know." They rode off with the girl's father,
sleepy and pleased, and Connie couldn't help but look
back at the darkened shopping plaza with its big empty
parking lot and its signs that were faded and ghostly
now, and over at the drive-in restaurant where cars
were still circling tirelessly. She couldn't hear the music
at this distance.

Next morning June asked her how the movie was
and Connie said, "So-so."

She and that girl and occasionally another girl
went out several times a week, and the rest of the time
Connie spent around the house—it was summer vaca-
tion—getting in her mother's way and thinking, dreaming about the boys she met. But all the boys fell back
and dissolved into a single face that was not even a face
but an idea, a feeling, mixed up with the urgent insistent pounding of the music and the humid night of
July. Connie's mother kept dragging her back to the
daylight by finding things for her to do or saying suddenly, "What's this about the Pettinger girl?"

And Connie would say nervously, "Oh, her. That
dope." She always drew thick clear lines between herself and such girls, and her mother was simple and
kind enough to believe it. Her mother was so simple,
Connie thought, that it was maybe cruel to fool her so
much. Her mother went scuffling around the house in
old bedroom slippers and complained over the telephone to one sister about the other, then the other
called up and the two of them complained about the
third one. If June's name was mentioned her mother's

tone was approving, and if Connie's name was mentioned it was disapproving. This did not really mean she disliked Connie, and actually Connie thought that her mother preferred her to June just because she was prettier, but the two of them kept up a pretense of exasperation, a sense that they were tugging and struggling over something of little value to either of them. Sometimes, over coffee, they were almost friends, but something would come up—some vexation that was like a fly buzzing suddenly around their heads—and their faces went hard with contempt.

One Sunday Connie got up at eleven—none of them bothered with church—and washed her hair so that it could dry all day long in the sun. Her parents and sister were going to a barbecue at an aunt's house and Connie said no, she wasn't interested, rolling her eyes to let her mother know just what she thought of it. "Stay home alone then," her mother said sharply. Connie sat out back in a lawn chair and watched them drive away, her father quiet and bald, hunched around so that he could back the car out, her mother with a look that was still angry and not at all softened through the windshield, and in the back seat poor old June, all dressed up as if she didn't know what a barbecue was, with all the running yelling kids and the flies. Connie sat with her eyes closed in the sun, dreaming and dazed with the warmth about her as if this were a kind of love, the caresses of love, and her mind slipped over onto thoughts of the boy she had been with the night before and how nice he had been, how sweet it always was, not the way someone like June would suppose but sweet, gentle, the way it was in movies and promised in songs; and when she opened her eyes she hardly knew where she was, the back yard ran off into weeds and a fence-like line of trees and behind it the sky was perfectly blue and still. The asbestos "ranch house" that was now three years old startled her—it looked small. She shook her head as if to get awake.

It was too hot. She went inside the house and turned on the radio to drown out the quiet. She sat on the edge of her bed, barefoot, and listened for an hour and a half to a program called XYZ Sunday Jamboree, record after record of hard, fast, shrieking songs she sang along with, interspersed by exclamations from "Bobby King": "An' look here, you girls at Napoleon's— Son and Charley want you to pay real close attention to this song coming up!"

And Connie paid close attention herself, bathed in a glow of slow-pulsed joy that seemed to rise mysteriously out of the music itself and lay languidly about the airless little room, breathed in and breathed out with each gentle rise and fall of her chest.

After a while she heard a car coming up the drive. She sat up at once, startled, because it couldn't be her father so soon. The gravel kept crunching all the way in from the road—the driveway was long—and Connie ran to the window. It was a car she didn't know. It was an open jalopy, painted a bright gold that caught the sunlight opaquely. Her heart began to pound and her fingers snatched at her hair, checking it, and she whispered, "Christ, Christ," wondering how bad she looked. The car came to a stop at the side door and the horn sounded four short taps, as if this were a signal Connie knew.

She went into the kitchen and approached the door slowly, then hung out the screen door, her bare toes curling down off the step. There were two boys in the car and now she recognized the driver: he had

shaggy, shabby black hair that looked crazy as a wig
and he was grinning at her.

"I ain't late, am I?" he said.

"Who the hell do you think you are?" Connie
said.

"Toldja I'd be out, didn't I?"

"I don't even know who you are."

She spoke sullenly, careful to show no interest or
pleasure, and he spoke in a fast, bright monotone. Connie looked past him to the other boy, taking her time.
He had fair brown hair, with a lock that fell onto his
forehead. His sideburns gave him a fierce, embarrassed
look, but so far he hadn't even bothered to glance at
her. Both boys wore sunglasses. The driver's glasses
were metallic and mirrored everything in miniature.

"You wanta come for a ride?" he said.

Connie smirked and let her hair fall loose over
one shoulder.

"Don'tcha like my car? New paint job," he said.
"Hey."

"What?"

"You're cute."

She pretended to fidget, chasing flies away from
the door.

"Don'tcha believe me, or what?" he said.

"Look, I don't even know who you are," Connie
said in disgust.

"Hey, Ellie's got a radio, see. Mine broke down."
He lifted his friend's arm and showed her the little transistor radio the boy was holding, and now Connie began
to hear the music. It was the same program that was
playing inside the house.

"Bobby King?" she said.

"I listen to him all the time. I think he's great."

"He's kind of great," Connie said reluctantly.

"Listen, that guy's *great*. He knows where the action is."

Connie blushed a little, because the glasses made it impossible for her to see just what this boy was looking at. She couldn't decide if she liked him or if he was just a jerk, and so she dawdled in the doorway and wouldn't come down or go back inside. She said, "What's all that stuff painted on your car?"

"Can'tcha read it?" He opened the door very carefully, as if he were afraid it might fall off. He slid out just as carefully, planting his feet firmly on the ground, the tiny metallic world in his glasses slowing down like gelatine hardening, and in the midst of it Connie's bright green blouse. "This here is my name, to begin with," he said. ARNOLD FRIEND was written in tarlike black letters on the side, with a drawing of a round, grinning face that reminded Connie of a pumpkin, except it wore sunglasses. "I wanta introduce myself, I'm Arnold Friend and that's my real name and I'm gonna be your friend, honey, and inside the car's Ellie Oscar, he's kinda shy." Ellie brought his transistor radio up to his shoulder and balanced it there. "Now, these numbers are a secret code, honey," Arnold Friend explained. He read off the numbers 33, 19, 17 and raised his eyebrows at her to see what she thought of that, but she didn't think much of it. The left rear fender had been smashed and around it was written, on the gleaming gold background: DONE BY CRAZY WOMAN DRIVER. Connie had to laugh at that. Arnold Friend was pleased at her laughter and looked up at her. "Around the other side's a lot more—you wanta come and seem them?"

"No."

"Why not?"

"Why should I?"

"Don'tcha wanta see what's on the car? Don'tcha wanta go for a ride?"

"I don't know."

"Why not?"

"I got things to do."

"Like what?"

"Things."

He laughed as if she had said something funny. He slapped his thighs. He was standing in a strange way, leaning back against the car as if he were balancing himself. He wasn't tall, only an inch or so taller than she would be if she came down to him. Connie liked the way he was dressed, which was the way all of them dressed: tight faded jeans stuffed into black, scuffed boots, a belt that pulled his waist in and showed how lean he was, and a white pullover shirt that was a little soiled and showed the hard small muscles of his arms and shoulders. He looked as if he probably did hard work, lifting and carrying things. Even his neck looked muscular. And his face was a familiar face, somehow: the jaw and chin and cheeks slightly darkened because he hadn't shaved for a day or two, and the nose long and hawklike, sniffing as if she were a treat he was going to gobble up and it was all a joke.

"Connie, you ain't telling the truth. This is your day set aside for a ride with me and you know it," he said, still laughing. The way he straightened and recovered from his fit of laughing showed that it had been all fake.

"How do you know what my name is?" she said suspiciously.

"It's Connie."

"Maybe and maybe not."

"I know my Connie," he said, wagging his finger. Now she remembered him even better, back at the restaurant, and her cheeks warmed at the thought of how she had sucked in her breath just at the moment she passed him—how she must have looked to him. And he had remembered her. "Ellie and I come out here especially for you," he said. "Ellie can sit in back. How about it?"

"Where?"

"Where what?"

"Where're we going?"

He looked at her. He took off the sunglasses and she saw how pale the skin around his eyes was, like holes that were not in shadow but instead in light. His eyes were like chips of broken glass that catch the light in an amiable way. He smiled. It was as if the idea of going for a ride somewhere, to someplace, was a new idea to him.

"Just for a ride, Connie sweetheart."

"I never said my name was Connie," she said.

"But I know what it is. I know your name and all about you, lots of things," Arnold Friend said. He had not moved yet but stood still leaning back against the side of his jalopy. "I took a special interest in you, such a pretty girl, and found out all about you—like I know your parents and sister are gone somewheres and I know where and how long they're going to be gone, and I know who you were with last night, and your best girl friend's name is Betty. Right?"

He spoke in a simple lilting voice, exactly as if he were reciting the words to a song. His smile assured her that everything was fine. In the car Ellie turned up the volume on his radio and did not bother to look around at them.

"Ellie can sit in the back seat," Arnold Friend said. He indicated his friend with a casual jerk of his chin, as if Ellie did not count and she should not bother with him.

"How'd you find out all that stuff?" Connie said.

"Listen: Betty Schultz and Tony Fitch and Jimmy Pettinger and Nancy Pettinger," he said in a chant. "Raymond Stanley and Bob Hutter—"

"Do you know all those kids?"

"I know everybody."

"Look, you're kidding. You're not from around here."

"Sure."

"But—how come we never saw you before?"

"Sure you saw me before," he said. He looked down at his boots, as if he were a little offended. "You just don't remember."

"I guess I'd remember you," Connie said.

"Yeah?" He looked up at this, beaming. He was pleased. He began to mark time with the music from Ellie's radio, tapping his fists lightly together. Connie looked away form his smile to the car, which was painted so bright it almost hurt her eyes to look at it. She looked at that name, ARNOLD FRIEND. And up at the front fender was an expression that was familiar—MAN THE FLYING SAUCERS. It was an expression kids had used the year before but didn't use this year. She looked at it for a while as if the words meant something to her that she did not yet know.

"What're you thinking about? Huh?" Arnold Friend demanded. "Not worried about your hair blowing around in the car, are you?"

"No."

"Think I maybe can't drive good?"

"How do I know?"

"You're a hard girl to handle. How come?" he said. "Don't you know I'm your friend? Didn't you see me put my sign in the air when you walked by?"

"What sign?"

"My sign." And he drew an X in the air, leaning out toward her. They were maybe ten feet apart. After his hand fell back to his side the X was still in the air, almost visible. Connie let the screen door close and stood perfectly still inside it, listening to the music from her radio and the boy's blend together. She stared at Arnold Friend. He stood there so stiffly relaxed, pretending to be relaxed, with one hand idly on the door handle as if he were keeping himself up that way and had no intention of ever moving again. She recognized most things about him, the tight jeans that showed his thighs and buttocks and the greasy leather boots and the tight shirt, and even that slippery friendly smile of his, that sleepy dreamy smile that all the boys used to get across ideas they didn't want to put into words. She recognized all this and also the singsong way he talked, slightly mocking, kidding, but serious and a little melancholy, and she recognized the way he tapped one fist against the other in homage to the perpetual music behind him. But all these things did not come together.

She said suddenly, "Hey, how old are you?"

His smile faded. She could see then that he wasn't a kid, he was much older—thirty, maybe more. At this knowledge her heart began to pound faster.

"That's a crazy thing to ask. Can'tcha see I'm your own age?"

"Like hell you are."

"Or maybe a coupla years older. I'm eighteen."

"Eighteen?" she said doubtfully.

He grinned to reassure her and lines appeared at the corners of his mouth. His teeth were big and white. He grinned so broadly his eyes became slits and she saw how thick the lashes were, thick and black as if painted with a black tarlike material. Then, abruptly, he seemed to become embarrassed and looked over his shoulder at Ellie. "*Him*, he's crazy," he said. "Ain't he a riot? He's a nut, a real character." Ellie was still listening to the music. His sunglasses told nothing about what he was thinking. He wore a bright orange shirt unbuttoned halfway to show his chest, which was a pale, bluish chest and not muscular like Arnold Friend's. His shirt collar was turned up all around and the very tips of the collar pointed out past his chin as if they were protecting him. He was pressing the transistor radio up against his ear and sat there in a kind of daze, right in the sun.

"He's kinda strange," Connie said.

"Hey, she says you're kinda strange! Kinda strange!" Arnold Friend cried. He pounded on the car to get Ellie's attention. Ellie turned for the first time and Connie saw with shock that he wasn't a kid either— he had a fair, hairless face, cheeks reddened slightly as if the veins grew too close to the surface of his skin, the face of a forty-year-old baby. Connie felt a wave of dizziness rise in her at this sight and she stared at him as if waiting for something to change the shock of the moment, make it all right again. Ellie's lips kept shaping words, mumbling along with the words blasting in his ear.

"Maybe you two better go away," Connie said faintly.

"What? How come?" Arnold Friend cried. "We come out here to take you for a ride. It's Sunday." He had the voice of the man on the radio now. It was the same voice, Connie thought: "Don'tcha know it's Sunday all day? And honey, no matter who you were with last night, today you're with Arnold Friend and don't you forget it! Maybe you better step out here," he said, and this last was in a different voice. It was a little flatter, as if the heat was finally getting to him.

"No. I got things to do."

"Hey."

"You two better leave."

"We ain't leaving until you come with us."

"Like hell I am—"

"Connie, don't fool around with me. I mean—I mean, don't fool *around*," he said, shaking his head. He laughed incredulously. He placed his sunglasses on top of his head, carefully, as if he were indeed wearing a wig, and brought the stems down behind his ears. Connie stared at him, another wave of dizziness and fear rising in her so that for a moment he wasn't even in focus but was just a blur standing there against his gold car, and she had the idea that he had driven up the driveway all right but had come from nowhere before that and belonged nowhere and that everything about him and even about the music that was so familiar to her was only half real.

"If my father comes and sees you—"

"He ain't coming. He's at a barbecue."

"How do you know that?"

"Aunt Tillie's. Right now they're—uh—they're drinking. Sitting around," he said vaguely, squinting as if he were staring all the way to town and over to Aunt Tillie's back yard. Then the vision seemed to get clear and he nodded energetically. "Yeah. Sitting around. There's your sister in a blue dress, huh? And high heels, the poor sad bitch—nothing like you, sweetheart! And your mother's helping some fat woman with the corn, they're cleaning the corn—husking the corn—"

"What fat woman?" Connie cried.

"How do I know what fat woman, I don't know every goddamn fat woman in the world!" Arnold Friend laughed.

"Oh, that's Mrs. Hornsby. . . . Who invited her?" Connie said. She felt a little lightheaded. Her breath was coming quickly.

"She's too fat. I don't like them fat. I like them the way you are, honey," he said, smiling sleepily at her. They stared at each other for a while through the screen door. He said softly, "Now, what you're going to do is this: you're going to come out that door. You're going to sit up front with me and Ellie's going to sit in the back, the hell with Ellie, right? This isn't Ellie's date. You're my date. I'm your lover, honey."

"What? You're crazy—"

"Yes, I'm your lover. You don't know what that is but you will," he said. "I know that too. I know all about you. But look: it's real nice and you couldn't ask for nobody better than me, or more polite. I always keep my word. I'll tell you how it is, I'm always nice at first, the first time. I'll hold you so tight you won't think you have to try to get away or pretend anything because you'll know you can't. And I'll come inside you where it's all secret and you'll give in to me and you'll love me—"

"Shut up! You're crazy!" Connie said. She backed away from the door. She put her hands up against her ears as if she'd heard something terrible, something not meant for her. "People don't talk like that, you're crazy," she muttered. Her heart was almost too big now for her chest and its pumping made sweat break out all over her. She looked out to see Arnold Friend pause and then take a step toward the porch, lurching. He almost fell. But, like clever drunken man, he managed to catch his balance. He wobbled in his high boots and grabbed hold of one of the porch posts.

"Honey?" he said. "You still listening?"

"Get the hell out of here!"

"Be nice, honey. Listen."

"I'm going to call the police—"

He wobbled again and out of the side of his mouth came a fast spat curse, an aside not meant for her to hear. But even this "Christ!" sounded forced. Then he began to smile again. She watched this smile come, awkward as if he were smiling from inside a mask. His whole face was a mask, she thought wildly, tanned down to his throat but then running out as if he had plastered makeup on his face but had forgotten about his throat.

"Honey—? Listen, here's how it is. I always tell the truth and I promise you this: I ain't coming in that house after you."

"You better not! I'm going to call the police if you—if you don't—"

"Honey," he said, talking right through her voice, "honey, I'm not coming in there but you are coming out here. You know why?"

She was panting. The kitchen looked like a place she had never seen before, some room she had run inside but that wasn't good enough, wasn't going to help her. The kitchen window had never had a curtain, after three years, and there were dishes in the sink for her to do—probably—and if you ran your hand across the table you'd probably feel something sticky there.

"You listening, honey? Hey?"

"—going to call the police—"

"Soon as you touch the phone I don't need to keep my promise and can come inside. You won't want that."

She rushed forward and tried to lock the door. Her fingers were shaking. "But why lock it," Arnold Friend said gently, talking right into her face. "It's just a screen door. It's just nothing." One of his boots was at a strange angle, as if his foot wasn't in it. It pointed out to the left, bent at the ankle. "I mean, anybody can break through a screen door and glass and wood and iron or anything else if he needs to, anybody at all, and specially Arnold Friend. If the place got lit up with a fire, honey, you'd come runnin' out into my arms, right into my arms an' safe at home—like you knew I was your lover and'd stopped fooling around." Part of those words were spoken with a slight rhythmic lilt, and Connie somehow recognized them—the echo of a song from last year, about a girl rushing into her boy friend's arms and coming home again—

Connie stood barefoot on the linoleum floor, staring at him. "What do you want?" she whispered.

"I want you," he said.

"What?"

"Seen you that night and thought, that's the one, yes sir. I never needed to look anymore."

"But my father's coming back. He's coming to get me. I had to wash my hair first—" She spoke in a dry, rapid voice, hardly raising it for him to hear.

"No, your daddy is not coming and yes, you had to wash your hair and you washed it for me. It's nice and shining and all for me. I thank you sweetheart," he said with a mock bow, but again he almost lost his balance. He had to bend and adjust his boots. Evidently

42

his feet did not go all the way down; the boots must have been stuffed with something so that he would seem taller. Connie stared out at him and behind him at Ellie in the car, who seemed to be looking off toward Connie's right, into nothing. This Ellie said, pulling the words out of the air one after another as if he were just discovering them, "You want me to pull out the phone?"

"Shut your mouth and keep it shut," Arnold Friend said, his face red from bending over or maybe from embarrassment because Connie had seen his boots. "This ain't none of your business."

"What—what are you doing? What do you want?" Connie said. "If I call the police they'll get you, they'll arrest you—"

"Promise was not to come in unless you touch that phone, and I'll keep that promise," he said. He resumed his erect position and tried to force his shoulders back. He sounded like a hero in a movie, declaring something important. But he spoke too loudly and it was as if he were speaking to someone behind Connie. "I ain't made plans for coming in that house where I don't belong but just for you to come out to me, the way you should. Don't you know who I am?"

"You're crazy," she whispered. She backed away from the door but did not want to go into another part of the house, as if this would give him permission to come through the door. "What do you . . . you're crazy, you. . . ."

"Huh? What're you saying, honey?"

Her eyes darted everywhere in the kitchen. She could not remember what it was, this room.

"This is how it is, honey: you come out and we'll drive away, have a nice ride. But if you don't come out we're gonna wait till your people come home and then they're all going to get it."

"You want that telephone pulled out?" Ellie said. He held the radio away from his ear and grimaced, as if without the radio the air was too much for him.

"I toldja shut up, Ellie," Arnold Friend said, "you're deaf, get a hearing aid, right? Fix yourself up. This little girl's no trouble and's gonna be nice to me, so Ellie keep to yourself, this ain't your date—right? Don't hem in on me, don't hog, don't crush, don't bird dog, don't trail me," he said in a rapid, meaningless voice, as if he were running through all the expressions he'd learned but was no longer sure which of them was in style, then rushing on to new ones, making them up with his eyes closed. "Don't crawl under my fence, don't squeeze in my chipmunk hole, don't sniff my glue, suck my popsicle, keep your own greasy fingers on yourself!" He shaded his eyes and peered in at Connie, who was backed against the kitchen table. "Don't mind him, honey, he's just a creep. He's a dope. Right? I'm the boy for you and like I said, you come out here nice like a lady and give me your hand, and nobody else gets hurt, I mean, your nice old bald-headed daddy and your mummy and your sister in her high heels. Because listen: why bring them in this?"

"Leave me alone," Connie whispered.

"Hey, you know that old woman down the road, the one with the chickens and stuff—you know her?"

"She's dead!"

"Dead? What? You know her?" Arnold Friend said.

"She's dead—"

"Don't you like her?"

"She's dead—she's —she isn't here any more—"

"But don't you like her, I mean, you got something against her? Some grudge or something?" Then his voice dipped as if he were conscious of a rudeness. He touched the sunglasses perched up on top of his head as if to make sure they were still there. "Now, you be a good girl."

"What are you going to do?"

"Just two things, or maybe three," Arnold Friend said. "But I promise it won't last long and you'll like me the way you get to like people you're close to. You will. It's all over for you here, so come on out. You don't want your people in any trouble, do you?"

She turned and bumped against a chair or something, hurting her leg, but she ran into the back room and picked up the telephone. Something roared in her ear, a tiny roaring, and she was so sick with fear that she could do nothing but listen to it—the telephone was clammy and very heavy and her fingers groped down to the dial but were too weak to touch it. She began to scream into the phone, into the roaring. She cried out, she cried for her mother, she felt her breath start jerking back and forth in her lungs as if it were something Arnold Friend was stabbing her with again and again with no tenderness. A noisy sorrowful wailing rose all about her and she was locked inside it the way she was locked inside this house.

After a while she could hear again. She was sitting on the floor with her wet back against the wall.

Arnold Friend was saying from the door, "That's a good girl. Put the phone back."

She kicked the phone away from her.

"No, honey. Pick it up. Put it back right."

She picked it up and put it back. The dial tone stopped.

"That's a good girl. Now, you come outside."

She was hollow with what had been fear but what was now just an emptiness. All that screaming had blasted it out of her. She sat, one leg cramped under her, and deep inside her brain was something like a pinpoint of light that kept going and would not let her relax. She thought, I'm not going to see my mother again. She thought, I'm not going to sleep in my bed again. Her bright green blouse was all wet.

Arnold Friend said, in a gentle-loud voice that was like a stage voice, "The place where you came from ain't there any more, and where you had in mind to go is cancelled out. This place you are now—inside your daddy's house—is nothing but a cardboard box I can knock down any time. You know that and always did know it. You hear me?"

She thought, I have got to think. I have got to know what to do.

"We'll go out to a nice field, out in the country here where it smells so nice and it's sunny," Arnold Friend said. "I'll have my arms tight around you so you won't need to try to get away and I'll show you what love is like, what it does. The hell with this house! It looks solid all right," he said. He ran a fingernail down the screen and the noise did not make Connie shiver, as it would have the day before. "Now, put your hand on your heart, honey. Feel that? That feels solid too but we know better. Be nice to me, be sweet like you can because what else is there for a girl like you but to be sweet and pretty and give in?—and get away before her people come back?"

She felt her pounding heart. Her hand seemed to enclose it. She thought for the first time in her life that it was nothing that was hers, that belonged to her, but just a pounding, living thing inside this body that wasn't really hers either.

"You don't want them to get hurt," Arnold Friend went on. "Now, get up, honey. Get up all by yourself."

She stood.

"Now, turn this way. That's right. Come over here to me.—Ellie, put that away, didn't I tell you? You dope. You miserable creepy dope," Arnold Friend said. His words were not angry but only part of an incantation. The incantation was kindly. "Now, come out through the kitchen to me, honey, and let's see a smile, try it, you're a brave, sweet little girl and now they're eating corn and hot dogs cooked to bursting over an outdoor fire, and they don't know one thing about you and never did and honey, you're better than them because not a one of them would have done this for you."

Connie felt the linoleum under her feet; it was cool. She brushed her hair back out of her eyes. Arnold Friend let go of the post tentatively and opened his arms for her, his elbows pointing in toward each other and his wrists limp, to show that this was an embarrassed embrace and a little mocking, he didn't want to make her self-conscious.

She put out her hand against the screen. She watched herself push the door slowly open as if she were back safe somewhere in the other doorway, watching this body and this head of long hair moving out into the sunlight where Arnold Friend waited.

"My sweet little blue-eyed girl," he said in a half-sung sigh that had nothing to do with her brown eyes but was taken up just the same by the vast sunlit reaches of the land behind him and on all sides of him—so much land that Connie had never seen before and did not recognize except to know that she was going to it.

❏ Background
to the Story

The Pied Piper of Tucson: He Cruised in a Golden Car, Looking for the Action

> Hey, c'mon babe, follow me,
> I'm the Pied Piper, follow me,
> I'm the Pied Piper,
> And I'll show you where it's at.
> —Popular song, Tucson, winter 1965

At dusk in Tucson, as the stark, yellow-flared mountains begin to blur against the sky, the golden car slowly cruises Speedway. Smoothly it rolls down the long, divided avenue, past the supermarkets, the gas stations and the motels; past the twist joints, the sprawling drive-in restaurants. The car slows for an intersection, stops, then pulls away again. The exhaust mutters against the pavement as the young man driving takes the machine swiftly, expertly through the gears. A car pulls even with him; the teenage girls in the front seat laugh, wave and call his name. The young man glances toward the rearview mirror, turned always so that he can look at his own reflection, and he appraises himself.

The face is his own creation: the hair dyed a raven black, the skin darkened to a deep tan with pancake make-up, the lips whitened, the whole effect heightened by a mole he has painted on one cheek. But the deep-set blue eyes are all his own. Beautiful eyes, the girls say.

From *Life* (March 4, 1966): 19–24, 80c–90.

51

Approaching the Hi-Ho, the teenagers' nightclub, he backs off on the accelerator, then slowly cruises on past Johnie's Drive-in. There the cars are beginning to orbit and accumulate in the parking lot—neat sharp cars with deep throated mufflers and Maltese-cross decals on the windows. But it's early yet. Not much going on. The driver shifts up again through the gears, and the golden car slides away along the glitter and gimcrack of Speedway. Smitty keeps looking for the action.

Whether the juries in the two trials decide that Charles Howard Schmid Jr. did or did not brutally murder Alleen Rowe, Gretchen Fritz and Wendy Fritz has from the beginning seemed of almost secondary importance to the people of Tucson. They are not indifferent. But what disturbs them far beyond the question of Smitty's guilt or innocence are the revelations about Tucson itself that have followed on the disclosure of the crimes. Starting with the bizarre circumstances of the killings and on through the ugly fragments of the plot—which in turn hint at other murders as yet undiscovered, at teenage sex, blackmail, even connections with the Cosa Nostra—they have had to view their city in a new and unpleasant light. The fact is that Charles Schmid—who cannot be dismissed as a freak, an aberrant of no consequence—had for years functioned successfully as a member, even a leader of the yeastiest stratum of Tucson's teenage society.

As a high school student Smitty had been, as classmates remember, an outsider—but not that far outside. He was small but he was a fine athlete, and in his last year—1960—he was a state gymnastics champion. His grades were poor, but he was in no trouble to speak of until his senior year, when he was suspended for stealing tools from a welding class.

But Smitty never really left the school. After his suspension he hung around waiting to pick up kids in a succession of sharp cars which he drove fast and well. He haunted all the teenage hangouts along Speedway, including the bowling alleys and the public swimming pool—and he put on spectacular diving exhibitions for girls far younger than he.

At the time of his arrest last November, Charles Schmid

was twenty-three years old. He wore face make-up and dyed his hair. He habitually stuffed three or four inches of old rags and tin cans into the bottoms of his high-topped boots to make himself taller than his five-foot-three and stumbled about so awkwardly while walking that some people thought he had wooden feet. He pursed his lips and let his eyelids droop in order to emulate his idol, Elvis Presley. He bragged to girls he knew a hundred ways to make love, that he ran dope, that he was a Hell's Angel. He talked about being a rough customer in a fight (he was, though he was rarely in one), and he always carried in his pocket tiny bottles of salt and pepper, which he said he used to blind his opponents. He liked to use highfalutin language and had a favorite saying, "I can manifest my neurotical emotions, emancipate an epicureal instinct, and elaborate on my heterosexual tendencies."

He occasionally shocked even those who thought they knew him well. A friend says he once saw Smitty tie a string to a tail of his pet cat, swing it around his head and beat it bloody against a wall. Then he turned calmly and asked, "You feel compassion—why?"

Yet even while Smitty tried to create an exalted, heroic image of himself, he had worked on a pitiable one. "He thrived on feeling sorry for himself," recalls a friend, "and making others feel sorry for him." At various times Smitty told intimates that he had leukemia and didn't have long to live. He claimed that he was adopted, that his real name was Angel Rodriguez, that his father was a "bean" (local slang for Mexican, an inferior race in Smitty's view), and that his mother was a famous lawyer who would have nothing to do with him.

What made Smitty a hero to Tucson's youth?

Isn't Tucson—out there in the Golden West, in the grand setting where the skies are not cloudy all day—supposed to be a flowering of the American Dream? One envisions teenagers who drink milk, wear crewcuts, go to bed at half past nine, say "Sir" and "Ma'am," and like to go fishing with Dad. Part of Tucson is like this—but the city is not yet Utopia. It is glass and chrome and well-weathered stucco; it is also gimcrack, ersatz and urban sprawl at its worst. Its suburbs stretch for mile after mile—a level sea of bungalows, broken only by mammoth shopping centers, that ultimately peters out among the cholla and saguaro. The city has grown from 85,000 to 300,000 since World War II. Few who live there were born there, and a lot are just passing through. Its superb climate attracts the old and the infirm, many of whom, as one citizen put it, "have come here to retire from their responsibilities to life." Jobs are hard to find and there is little industry to stabilize employment. ("What do people do in Tucson?" the visitor asks. Answer: "They do each others' laundry.")

As for the youngsters, they must compete with the army of semi-retired who are willing to take on part-time work for the minimum wage. Schools are beautiful but overcrowded; and at those with split sessions, the kids are on the loose from noon on, or from six p.m. till noon the next day. When they get into trouble, Tucson teenagers are capable of getting into trouble in style: a couple of years ago they shocked the city fathers by throwing a series of beer-drinking parties in the desert, attended by scores of kids. The fests were called "boondockers" and if they were no more sinful than any other kids' drinking parties, they were at least on a magnificent scale. One statistic seems relevant: fifty runaways are reported to the Tucson police department each month.

Of an evening kids with nothing to do wind up on Speedway, looking for action. There is the teenage nightclub ("Pickup Palace," the kids call it). There are rock 'n' roll beer joints (the owners check ages meticulously, but young girls can enter if they don't drink; besides, anyone can buy a phony I.D. card for $2.50 around the high schools) where they can Jerk, Swim and Frug away the evening to the room-shaking electronic blare of "Hang On Sloopy," "The Pied Piper," and a number called "The Bo Diddley Rock." At the drive-in hamburger and pizza stands their cars circle endlessly, mufflers rumbling, as they check each other over.

Here on Speedway you find Richie and Ronny, out of work and bored with nothing to do. Here you find Debby and Jabron, from the wrong side of the tracks, aimlessly cruising in their battered old car looking for something—anything—to relieve the tedium of their lives, looking for somebody neat. ("Well if the boys look bitchin', you pull up next to them in your car and you roll down the window and say, 'Hey, how

54

about a dollar for gas?' and if they give you the dollar then maybe you let them take you to Johnie's for a Coke.") Here you find Gretchen, pretty and rich and with problems, bad problems. Of a Saturday night, all of them cruising the long, bright street that seems endlessly in motion with the young. Smitty's people.

He had a nice car. He had plenty of money from his parents, who ran a nursing home, and he was always glad to spend it on anyone who'd listen to him. He had a pad of his own where he threw parties and he had impeccable manners. He was always willing to help a friend and he would send flowers to girls who were ill. He was older and more mature than most of his friends. He knew where the action was, and if he wore makeup—well, at least he was *different*.

Some of the older kids—those who worked, who had something else to do—thought Smitty was a creep. But to the youngsters—to the bored and the lonely, to the dropout and the delinquent, to the young girls with beehive hairdos and tight pants they didn't quite fill out, and to the boys with acne and no jobs—to these people, Smitty was a kind of folk hero. Nutty maybe, but at least more dramatic, more theatrical, more *interesting* than anyone else in their lives: a semi-ludicrous, sexy-eyed pied-piper who, stumbling along in his rag-stuffed boots, led them up and down Speedway.

On the evening of May 31, 1964, Alleen Rowe prepared to go to bed early. She had to be in class by six a.m. and she had an examination the next day. Alleen was a pretty girl of fifteen, a better-than-average student who talked about going to college and becoming an oceanographer. She was also a sensitive child—given to reading romantic novels and taking long walks in the desert at night. Recently she had been going through a period of adolescent melancholia, often talking with her mother, a nurse, about death. She would, she hoped, be some day reincarnated as a cat.

On this evening, dressed in a black bathing suit and thongs, her usual costume around the house, she had watched the Beatles on TV and had tried to teach her mother to dance the Frug. Then she took her bath, washed her hair, and came out to kiss her mother good night. Norma Rowe, an attractive, womanly divorcée, was somehow moved by the girl's clean fragrance and said, "You smell so good—are you wearing perfume?"

"No, Mom," the girl answered, laughing, "it's just me."

A little later Mrs. Rowe looked in on her daughter, found her apparently sleeping peacefully, and then left for her job as a night nurse in a Tucson hospital. She had no premonition of danger, but she had lately been concerned about Alleen's friendship with a neighbor girl named Mary French.

Mary and Alleen had been spending a good deal of time together, smoking and giggling and talking girl talk in the Rowe backyard. Norma Rowe did not approve. She particularly did not approve of Mary French's friends, a tall, gangling boy of nineteen named John Saunders and another named Charles Schmid. She had seen Smitty racing up and down the street in his car and once, when he came to call on Alleen and found her not at home, he had looked at Norma so menacingly with his "pinpoint eyes" that she had been frightened.

Her daughter, on the other hand, seemed to have mixed feelings about Smitty. "He's creepy," she once told her mother, "he just makes me crawl. But he can be nice when he wants to."

At any rate, later that night—according to Mary French's sworn testimony—three friends arrived at Alleen Rowe's house: Smitty, Mary French, and Saunders. Smitty had frequently talked with Mary French about killing the Rowe girl by hitting her over the head with a rock. Mary French tapped on Alleen's window and asked her to come out and drink beer with them. Wearing a shift over her bathing suit, she came willingly enough.

Schmid's two accomplices were strange and pitiable creatures. Each of them was afraid of Smitty, yet each was drawn to him. As a baby, John Saunders had been so afflicted with allergies that scabs encrusted his entire body. To keep him from scratching himself his parents had tied his hands and feet to the crib each night, and when eventually he was cured he was so conditioned that he could not go to sleep without being bound hand and foot.

Later, a scrawny boy with poor eyesight ("Just a skinny little body with a big head on it"), he was taunted and bullied by larger children; in turn he bullied those who were smaller. He also suffered badly from asthma and he had few friends. In high school he was a poor student and constantly in minor trouble.

Mary French, nineteen, was—to put it straight—a frump. Her face, which might have been pretty, seemed somehow lumpy, her body shapeless. She was not dull but she was always a poor student, and she finally had simply stopped going to high school. She was, a friend remembers, "fantastically in love with Smitty. She just sat home and waited while he went out with other girls."

Now, with Smitty at the wheel, the four teen-agers headed for the desert, which begins out Golf Links Road. It is spooky country, dry and empty, the yellow sand clotted with cholla and mesquite and stunted, strangely green palo verde trees, and the great humanoid saguaro that hulk against the sky. Out there at night you can hear the yip and ki-yi of coyotes, the piercing screams of wild creatures—cats, perhaps.

According to Mary French, they got out of the car and walked down into a wash, where they sat on the sand and talked for a while, the four of them. Schmid and Mary then started back to the car. Before they got there, they heard a cry and Schmid turned back toward the wash. Mary went on to the car and sat in it alone. After forty-five minutes, Saunders appeared and said Smitty wanted her to come back down. She refused, and Saunders went away. Five or ten minutes later, Smitty showed up. "He got into the car," says Mary, "and he said, 'We killed her. I love you very much.' He kissed me. He was breathing real hard and seemed excited." Then Schmid got a shovel from the trunk of the car and they returned to the wash. "She was lying on her back and there was blood on her face and head," Mary French testified. Then the three of them dug a shallow grave and put the body in it covered it up. Afterwards, they wiped Schmid's car clean of Alleen's fingerprints.

More than a year passed. Norma Rowe had reported her daughter missing and the police searched for her—after a fashion. At Mrs. Rowe's insistence they picked up Schmid, but they had no reason to hold him. The police, in fact, assumed that Alleen was just one more of Tucson's runaways.

Norma Rowe, however, had become convinced that Alleen had been killed by Schmid, although she left her kitchen light on every night in case Alleen did come home. She badgered the police and she badgered the sheriff until the authorities began to dismiss her as a crank. She began to imagine a high-level conspiracy against her. She wrote the state attorney general, the FBI, the U.S. Department of Health, Education and Welfare. She even contacted a New Jersey mystic, who said she could see Alleen's body out in the desert under a big tree.

Ultimately Norma Rowe started her own investigation, questioning Alleen's friends, poking around, dictating her findings to a tape recorder; she even tailed Smitty at night, following him in her car, scared stiff that he might spot her.

Schmid, during this time, acquired a little house of his own. There he held frequent parties, where people sat around amid his stacks of *Playboy* magazines, playing Elvis Presley records and drinking beer.

He read Jules Feiffer's novel, *Harry, the Rat with Women,* and said that his ambition was to be like Harry and have a girl commit suicide over him. Once, according to a friend, he went to see a minister, who gave him a Bible and told him to read the first three chapters of John. Instead Schmid tore the pages out and burned them in the street. "Religion is a farce," he announced. He started an upholstery business with some friends, called himself "founder and president," but then failed to put up the money he promised and the venture was short-lived.

He decided he liked blondes best, and took to dyeing the hair of various teenage girls he went around with. He went out and bought two imitation diamonds for about $13 apiece and then engaged himself, on the same day, both to Mary French and to a fifteen-year-old girl named Kathy Morath. His plan, he confided to a friend, was to put each of the girls to work and have them deposit their salaries in a bank account held jointly with him. Mary French did indeed go to work in the convalescent home Smitty's parents operated. When their bank account was fat enough, Smitty withdrew the money and bought a tape recorder.

By this time Smitty also had a girl from a higher social stratum than he usually was involved with. She was Gretchen Fritz, daughter of a prominent Tucson heart surgeon. Gretchen was a pretty, thin, nervous girl of seventeen with a knack for trouble. A teacher described her as "erratic, subversive, a psychopathic liar."

At the horsy private school she attended for a time she was a misfit. She not only didn't care about horses, but she shocked her classmates by telling them they were foolish for going out with boys without getting paid for it. Once she even committed the unpardonable social sin of turning up at a formal dance party accompanied by boys wearing what was described as beatnik dress. She cut classes, she was suspected of stealing and when, in the summer before her senior year, she got into trouble with juvenile authorities for her role in an attempted theft at a liquor store, the headmaster suggested she not return and then recommended she get psychiatric treatment.

Charles Schmid saw Gretchen for the first time at a public swimming pool in the summer of 1964. He met her by the simple expedient of following her home, knocking on the door and, when she answered, saying, "Don't I know you?" They talked for an hour. Thus began a fierce and stormy relationship. A good deal of what authorities know of the development of this relationship comes from the statements of a spindly scarecrow of a young man who wears pipestem trousers and Beatle boots: Richard Bruns. At the time Smitty was becoming involved with Gretchen, Bruns was eighteen years old. He had served two terms in the reformatory at Fort Grant. He had been in and out of trouble all his life, had never fit in anywhere. Yet, although he never went beyond the tenth grade in school and his credibility on many counts is suspect, he is clearly intelligent and even sensitive. He was, for a time, Smitty's closest friend and confidant, and he is today one of the mainstays of the state's case against Smitty. His story:

He and Gretchen were always fighting," says Bruns. "She didn't want him to drink or go out with the guys or go out with other girls. She wanted him to stay home, call her on the phone, be punctual. First she would get suspicious of him, then he'd get suspicious of her. They were made for each other."

Their mutual jealousy led to sharp and continual arguments. Once she infuriated him by throwing a bottle of shoe polish on his car. Another time she was driving past Smitty's house and saw him there with some other girls. She jumped out of her car and began screaming. Smitty took off into the house, out the back, and climbed a tree in his backyard.

His feelings for her were an odd mixture of hate and adoration. He said he was madly in love with her, but he called her a whore. She would let Smitty in her bedroom window at night. Yet he wrote an anonymous letter to the Tucson Health Department accusing her of having venereal disease and spreading it about town. But Smitty also went to enormous lengths to impress Gretchen, once shooting holes through the windows of his car and telling her that thugs, from whom he was protecting her, had fired at him. So Bruns described the relationship.

On the evening of August 16, 1965 Gretchen Fritz left the house with her little sister Wendy, a friendly, lively thirteen-year-old, to go to a drive-in movie. Neither girl ever came home again. Gretchen's father, like Alleen Rowe's mother, felt sure that Charles Schmid had something to do with his daughters' disappearance, and eventually he hired Bill Heilig, a private detective, to handle the case. One of Heilig's men soon found Gretchen's red compact car parked behind a motel, but the police continued to assume that the girls had joined the ranks of Tucson's runaways.

About a week after Gretchen disappeared, Bruns was at Smitty's home. "We were sitting in the living room," Bruns recalls. "He was sitting on the sofa and I was in the chair by the window and we got on the subject of Gretchen. He said, 'You know I killed her?' I said I didn't, and he said, 'You know where?' I said no. He said, 'I did it here in the living room. First I killed Gretchen, then Wendy was still going "*huh, huh, huh,*" so I . . . [here Bruns showed how Smitty made a garroting gesture.] Then I took the bodies and put them in the trunk of the car. I put the bodies in the most obvious place I could think of because I just didn't care any more. Then I ditched the car and wiped it clean."

Bruns was not particularly upset by Smitty's story. Months before, Smitty had told him of the murder of Alleen Rowe, and nothing had come of that. So he was not certain Smitty was telling the truth about the Fritz girls. Besides, Bruns detested Gretchen himself. But what happened next, still according to Bruns's story, did shake him up.

One night not long after, a couple of tough-looking characters, wearing sharp suits and smoking cigars, came by with Smitty and picked up Bruns. Smitty said they were Mafia, and that someone had hired them to look for Gretchen. Smitty and Bruns were taken to an apartment where several men were present whom Smitty later claimed to have recognized as local Cosa Nostra figures.

They wanted to know what had happened to the girls. They made no threats, but the message, Bruns remembers, came across loud and clear. These were no street-corner punks: these were the real boys. In spite of the intimidating company, Schmid lost none of his insouciance. He said he didn't know where Gretchen was, but if she turned up hurt he wanted these men to help him get whoever was responsible. He added that he thought she might have gone to California.

By the time Smitty and Bruns got back to Smitty's house, they were both a little shaky. Later that night, says Bruns, Smitty did the most unlikely thing imaginable: he called the FBI. First he tried the Tucson office and couldn't raise anyone. Then he called Phoenix and couldn't get an agent there either. Finally he put in a person-to-person call to J. Edgar Hoover in Washington. He didn't get Hoover, of course, but he got someone and told him that the Mafia was harassing him over the disappearance of a girl. The FBI promised to have someone in touch with him soon.

Bruns was scared and said so. It occurred to him now that if Smitty really had killed the Fritz girls and left their bodies in an obvious place, they were in very bad trouble indeed—with the Mafia on one hand and the FBI on the other. "Let's go bury them," Bruns said.

"Smitty stole the keys to his old man's station wagon," says Bruns, "and then we got a flat shovel—the only one we could find. We went to Johnie's and got a hamburger, and then we drove out to the old drinking spot [in the desert]—that's what Smitty meant when he said the most obvious place. It's where we used to drink beer and make out with girls.

"So we parked the car and got the shovel and walked down there, and we couldn't find anything. Then Smitty said, 'Wait, I smell something.' We went in opposite directions looking, and then I heard Smitty say, 'Come here.' I found him kneeling over Gretchen. There was a white rag tied around her legs. Her blouse was pulled up and she was wearing a white bra and Capris.

"Then he said, 'Wendy's up this way.' I sat there for a minute. Then I followed Smitty to where Wendy was. He'd had the decency to cover her—except for one leg, which was sticking up out of the ground.

"We tried to dig with the flat shovel. We each took turns. He'd dig for a while and then I'd dig for a while, but the ground was hard and we couldn't get anywhere with that flat shovel. We dug for twenty minutes and finally Smitty said we'd better do something because it's going to get light. So he grabbed the rag that was around Gretchen's legs and dragged her down in the wash. It made a noise like dragging a hollow shell. It stunk like hell. Then Smitty said wipe off her shoes, there might be fingerprints, so I wiped them off with my handkerchief and threw it away.

"We went back to Wendy. Her leg was sticking up with a shoe on it. He said take off her tennis shoe and throw it over there. I did, I threw it. Then he said, 'Now you're in this as deep as I am.'" By then, the sisters had been missing for about two weeks.

Early next morning Smitty did see the FBI. Nevertheless—here Bruns's story grows even wilder—that same day Smitty left for California, accompanied by a couple of Mafia types, to look for Gretchen Fritz. While there, he was picked up by the San Diego police on a complaint that he was impersonating an FBI officer. He was detained briefly, released and then returned to Tucson.

But now, it seemed to Richard Bruns, Smitty began acting very strangely. He startled Bruns by saying, "I've killed—

not three times, but four. Now it's your turn, Richie." He went beserk in his little house, smashing his fist through a wall, slamming doors, then rushing out into the backyard in nothing but his undershorts, when he ran through the night screaming, "God is going to punish me!" He also decided, suddenly, to get married—to a fifteen-year-old girl who was a stranger to most of his friends.

If Smitty seemed to Bruns to be losing his grip, Richie Bruns himself was not in much better shape. His particular quirk revolved around Kathy Morath, the thin, pretty, sixteen-year-old daughter of a Tucson postman. Kathy had once been attracted to Smitty. He had given her one of his two cut-glass engagement rings. But Smitty never really took her seriously, and one day, in a fit of pique and jealousy, she threw the ring back in his face. Richie Bruns comforted her and then started dating for himself. He was soon utterly and irrevocably smitten with goofy adoration.

Kathy accepted Bruns as a suitor, but halfheartedly. She thought him weird (oddly enough, she did not think Smitty in the least weird) and their romance was short-lived. After she broke up with him last July, Bruns went into a blue funk, a nosedive into romantic melancholy, and then, like some love-swacked Elizabethan poet, he started pouring out his heart to her on paper. He sent her poems, short stories, letters twenty-four pages long. ("My God, you should have read the stuff," says her perplexed father. "His letters were so romantic it was like 'Next week, East Lynne.'") Bruns even began writing a novel dedicated to "My Darling Kathy."

If Bruns had confined himself to literary catharsis, the murders of the Rowe and Fritz girls might never have been disclosed. But Richie went a little bit around the bend. He became obsessed with the notion that Kathy Morath was the next victim on Smitty's list. Someone had cut the Moraths' screen door, there had been a prowler around her house, and Bruns was sure that it was Smitty. (Kathy and her father, meantime, were sure it was Bruns.)

"I started having this dream," Bruns says. "It was the same dream every night. Smitty would have Kathy out in the desert and he'd be doing all those things to her, and strangling her, and I'd be running across the desert with a gun in my hand, but I could never get there."

If Bruns couldn't save Kathy in his dreams, he could, he figured, stop a walking, breathing Smitty. His scheme for doing so was so wild and so simple that it put the whole Morath family into a state of panic and very nearly landed Bruns in jail.

Bruns undertook to stand guard over Kathy Morath. He kept watch in front of her house, in the alley, and in the street. He patrolled the sidewalk from early in the morning till late at night, seven days a week. If Kathy was home he would be there. If she went out, he would follow her. Kathy's father called the police, and when they told Bruns he couldn't loiter around like that, Bruns fetched his dog and walked the animal up and down the block, hour after hour.

Bruns by now was wallowing in feelings of sacrifice and nobility—all of it unappreciated by Kathy Morath and her parents. At the end of October, he was finally arrested for harassing the Morath family. The judge facing the obviously woebegone and smitten young man, told Bruns that he wouldn't be jailed if he'd agree to get out of town until he got over his infatuation.

Bruns agreed and a few days later went to Ohio to stay with his grandmother and to try to get a job. It was hopeless. He couldn't sleep at night, and if he did doze off he had his old nightmare again.

One night he blurted out the whole story to his grandmother in their kitchen. She thought he had had too many beers and didn't believe him. "I hear beer does strange things to a person," she said comfortingly. At her words Bruns exploded, knocked over a chair and shouted, "The one time in my life when I need advice what do I get?" A few minutes later he was on the phone to the Tucson police.

Things happened swiftly. At Bruns's frantic insistence, the police picked up Kathy Morath and put her in protective custody. They went into the desert and discovered—precisely as Bruns had described them—the grisly, skeletal remains of Gretchen and Wendy Fritz. They started the machinery that resulted in the arrest a week later of John Saunders and Mary

French. They found Charles Schmid working in the yard of his little house, his face layered with make-up, his nose covered by a patch of adhesive plaster which he had worn for five months, boasting that his nose was broken in a fight, and his boots packed full of old rags and tin cans. He put up no resistance.

John Saunders and Mary French confessed immediately to their roles in the slaying of Alleen Rowe and were quickly sentenced, Mary French to four to five years, Saunders to life. When Smitty goes on trial for this crime, on March 15, they will be principal witnesses against him.

Meanwhile Richie Bruns, the perpetual misfit, waits apprehensively for the end of the Fritz trial, desperately afraid that Schmid will go free. "If he does," Bruns says glumly, "I'll be the first one he'll kill."

As for Charles Schmid, he has adjusted well to his period of waiting. He is polite and agreeable with all, though at the preliminary hearings he glared menacingly at Richie Bruns. Dressed tastefully, tie neatly knotted, hair carefully combed, his face scrubbed clean of make-up, he is a short, compact, darkly handsome young man with a wide, engaging smile and those deepset eyes.

The people of Tucson wait uneasily for what fresh scandal the two trials may develop. Civic leaders publicly cry that a slur has been cast on their community by an isolated crime. High school students have held rallies and written vehement editorials in the school papers, protesting that they are all being judged by the actions of a few oddballs and misfits. But the city reverberates with stories of organized teen-age crime and vice, in which Smitty is cast in the role of a minor-league underworld boss. None of these later stories has been substantiated.

One disclosure, however, has most disturbing implications: Smitty's boasts may have been heard not just by Bruns and his other intimates, but by other teen-agers as well. How many—and precisely how much they knew—it remains impossible to say. One authoritative source, however, having listened to the admissions of six high school students, says they unquestionably knew enough so that they should have gone to the police—but were either afraid to talk, or didn't want to rock the boat. As for Smitty's friends, the thought of telling the police never entered their minds.

"I didn't know he killed her," said one, "and even if I had, I wouldn't have said anything. I wouldn't want to be a fink."

Out in the respectable Tucson suburbs parents have started to crack down on the youngsters and have declared Speedway hangouts off limits. "I thought my folks were bad before," laments one grounded sixteen-year-old, "but now they're just impossible."

As for the others—Smitty's people—most don't care very much. Things are duller without Smitty around, but things have always been dull.

"There's nothing to do in this town," says one of his girls, shaking her dyed blond hair. "The only other town I know is Las Vegas and there's nothing to do there either." For her, and for her friends, there's nothing to do in any town.

They are down on Speedway again tonight, cruising, orbiting the drive-ins, stopping by the joints, where the words of "The Bo Diddley Rock" cut through the smoke and the electronic dissonance like some macabre reminder of their fallen hero:

> All you women stand in line,
> And I'll love you all in an hour's time. . . .
> I got a cobra snake for a neck-tie,
> I got a brand-new house on the roadside
> Covered with rattlesnake hide,
> I got a brand-new chimney made on top,
> Made out of human skulls.
> Come on baby, take a walk with me,
> And tell me, who do you love?
> Who do you love?
> Who do you love?
> Who do you love?

"Where Are You Going, Where Have You Been?" and *Smooth Talk:* Short Story into Film

Some years ago in the American Southwest there surfaced a tabloid psychopath known as "The Pied Piper of Tucson." I have forgotten his name, but his specialty was the seduction and occasional murder of teen-aged girls. He may or may not have had actual accomplices, but his bizarre activities were known among a circle of teenagers in the Tucson area; for some reason they kept his secret, deliberately did not inform parents or police. It was this fact, not the fact of the mass murderer himself, that struck me at the time. And this was a pre-Manson time, early or mid-1960s.

The Pied Piper mimicked teenagers in their talk, dress, and behavior, but he was not a teenager—he was a man in his early thirties. Rather short, he stuffed rags in his leather boots to give himself height. (And sometimes walked unsteadily as a consequence: did none among his admiring constituency notice?) He charmed his victims as charismatic psychopaths have always charmed their victims, to the bewilderment of others who fancy themselves free of all lunatic attractions. The Pied Piper of Tucson: a trashy dream, a tabloid archetype, sheer artifice, comedy, cartoon—surrounded, however

From *(Woman) Writer: Occasions and Opportunities* (New York: E. P. Dutton, 1988).

67

improbably, and finally tragically, by real people. You think that, if you look twice, he won't be there. But there he is.

I don't remember any longer where I first read about this Pied Piper—very likely in *Life* Magazine. I do recall deliberately not reading the full article because I didn't want to be distracted by too much detail. It was not after all the mass murderer himself who intrigued me, but the disturbing fact that a number of teenagers—from "good" families—aided and abetted his crimes. This is the sort of thing authorities and responsible citizens invariably call "inexplicable" because they can't find explanations for it. *They* would not have fallen under this maniac's spell, after all.

An early draft of my short story "Where Are You Going, Where Have You Been?"—from which the film *Smooth Talk* was adapted by Joyce Chopra and Tom Cole—had the rather too explicit title "Death and the Maiden." It was cast in a mode of fiction to which I am still partial—indeed, every third or fourth story of mine is probably in this mode—"realistic allegory," it might be called. It is Hawthornean, romantic, shading into parable. Like the medieval German engraving from which my title was taken, the story was minutely detailed yet clearly an allegory of the fatal attractions of death (or the devil). An innocent young girl is seduced by way of her own vanity; she mistakes death for erotic romance of a particularly American/ trashy sort.

In subsequent drafts the story changed in tone, its focus, its language, its title. It became "Where Are You Going, Where Have You Been?" Written at a time when the author was intrigued by the music of Bob Dylan, particularly the hauntingly elegiac song "It's All Over Now, Baby Blue," it was dedicated to Bob Dylan. The charismatic mass murderer drops into the background and his innocent victim, a fifteen-year-old, moves into the foreground. She becomes the true protagonist of the tale, courting and being courted by her fate, a self-styled 1950s pop figure, alternately absurd and winning. There is no suggestion in the published story that "Arnold Friend" has seduced and murdered other young girls, or even that he necessarily intends to murder Connie. Is his interest "merely" sexual? (Nor is there anything about the complicity

68

of other teenagers. I saved that yet more provocative note for a current story, "Testimony.") Connie is shallow, vain, silly, hopeful, doomed—but capable nonetheless of an unexpected gesture of heroism at the story's end. Her smooth-talking seducer, who cannot lie, promises her that her family will be unharmed if she gives herself to him; and so she does. The story ends abruptly at the point of her "crossing over." We don't know the nature of her sacrifice, only that she is generous enough to make it.

In adapting a narrative so spare and thematically foreshortened as "Where Are You Going, Where Have You Been?" film director Joyce Chopra and screenwriter Tom Cole were required to do a good deal of filling in, expanding, inventing. Connie's story becomes lavishly, and lovingly, textured; she is not an allegorical figure so much as a "typical" teenaged girl (if Laura Dern, spectacularly good-looking, can be so defined). Joyce Chopra, who has done documentary films on contemporary teenage culture and, yet more authoritatively, has an adolescent daughter of her own, creates in *Smooth Talk* a vivid and absolutely believable world for Connie to inhabit. Or worlds: as in the original story there is Connie-at-home, and there is Connie-with-her-friends. Two fifteen-year-old girls, two finely honed styles, two voices, sometimes but not often overlapping. It is one of the marvelous visual features of the film that we *see* Connie and her friends transform themselves, once they are safely free of parental observation. The girls claim their true identities in the neighborhood shopping mall. What freedom, what joy!

Smooth Talk is, in a way, as much Connie's mother's story as it is Connie's; its center of gravity, its emotional nexus, is frequently with the mother—warmly and convincingly played by Mary Kay Place. (Though the mother's sexual jealousy of her daughter is slighted in the film.) Connie's ambiguous relationship with her affable, somewhat mysterious father (well played by Levon Helm) is an excellent touch: I had thought, subsequent to the story's publication, that I should have built up the father, suggesting, as subtly as I could, an attraction there paralleling the attraction Connie feels for

Laura Dern as Connie in *Smooth Talk* (1986). Courtesy of the Museum of Modern Art/Film Stills Archive

her seducer, Arnold Friend. And Arnold Friend himself—"A. Friend" as he says—is played with appropriately overdone sexual swagger by Treat Williams, who is perfect for the part; and just the right age. We see that Arnold Friend isn't a teenager even as Connie, mesmerized by his presumed charm, does not seem to *see* him at all. What is so difficult to accom-

plish in prose—nudging the reader to look over the protagonist's shoulder, so to speak—is accomplished with enviable ease
in film.

Treat Williams as Arnold Friend is supreme in his very
awfulness, as, surely, the original Pied Piper of Tucson must
have been. (Though no one involved in the film knew about
the original source.) Mr. Williams flawlessly impersonates
Arnold Friend as Arnold Friend impersonates—is it James
Dean? James Dean regarding himself in mirrors, doing James
Dean impersonations? That Connie's fate is so trashy is in fact
her fate.

What is outstanding in Joyce Chopra's *Smooth Talk* is its visual freshness, its sense of motion and life; the attentive intelligence the director has brought to the semi-secret world of
the American adolescent—shopping mall flirtations, drive-in
restaurant romances, highway hitchhiking, the fascination of
rock music played very, very loud. (James Taylor's music for
the film is wonderfully appropriate. We hear it as Connie hears
it; it is the music of her spiritual being.) Also outstanding, as I
have indicated, and numerous critics have noted, are the acting performances. Laura Dern is so dazzlingly right as "my"
Connie that I may come to think I modeled the fictitious girl
on her, in the way that writers frequently delude themselves
about motions of causality.

My difficulties with *Smooth Talk* have primarily to do
with my chronic hesitation—about seeing/hearing work of
mine abstracted from its contexture of language. All writers
know that language is their subject; quirky word choices, patterns of rhythm, enigmatic pauses, punctuation marks. Where
the quick scanner sees "quick" writing, the writer conceals
nine tenths of the iceberg. Of course we all have "real" subjects, but beneath the tale-telling it is the tale-telling that grips
us so very fiercely. The writer works in a single dimension, the
director works in three. I assume they are professionals to
their fingertips; authorities in their medium as I am an authority (if I am) in mine. I would fiercely defend the place-
ment of a semicolon in one of my novels but I would probably
have deferred in the end to Joyce Chopra's decision to reverse
the story's conclusion, turn it upside down, in a sense, so that

71

the film ends not with death, not with a sleepwalker's crossing over to her fate, but upon a scene of reconciliation, rejuvenation.

A girl's loss of virginity, bittersweet but not necessarily tragic. Not today. A girl's coming-of-age that involves her succumbing to, but then rejecting the "trashy dreams" of her pop teenage culture. "Where Are You Going, Where Have You Been?" defines itself as allegorical in its conclusion: Death and Death's chariot (a funky souped-up convertible) have come for the Maiden. Awakening is, in the story's final lines, moving out into the sunlight where Arnold Friend waits:

> "My sweet little blue-eyed girl," he said in a half-sung sigh that had nothing to do with [Connie's] brown eyes but was taken up just the same by the vast sunlit reaches of the land behind him and on all sides of him—so much land that Connie had never seen before and did not recognize except to know that she was going to it.

—a conclusion impossible to transfigure into film.

Critical Essays

☐ MARIE MITCHELL OLESON URBANSKI ■

Existential Allegory: Joyce Carol Oates's "Where Are You Going, Where Have You Been?"

Fifteen-year-old Connie's acquiescences to Arnold Friend's threat-ridden seduction is an appropriate finale to Joyce Carol Oates's "Where Are You Going, Where Have You Been?" in a narrative which, upon careful analysis, suggests existential allegory. Many critics have classified Oates's work as realistic or naturalistic, whereas Samuel J. Pickering categorizes her short stories as subjective romanticism to a fault.[1] Most, however, agree she is writing in the tradition of Dreiser, Faulkner, and O'Connor, but few have acknowledged the allegorical nature of her work. Veiling the intent of "Where Are You Going . . ." in realistic detail, Oates sets up the framework of a religious allegory—the seduction of Eve—and with it renders a contemporary existential initiation theme—that of a young person coming to grips with externally determined fate.

The first paragraph introduces the vain, spoiled daughter of middle-class parents, "She knew she was pretty and that was everything." The sense of power which her fresh desirable sexuality provides her is the basis for her feeling of a self-directed life. When she and her girlfriend visit a local "hangout" and reject the overtures of an undesirable boy, "it made them feel good to be able to ignore him."

From *Studies in Short Fiction* 15 (1978): 200–203.

From the outset of the narrative, members of Connie's family recognize their powerlessness and thus their difference from her. Her mother and sister are not attractive, so they do not really count; and her father, who spends most of his time at work, is weak. Rose Marie Burwell's interpretation of *A Garden of Earthly Delights* as moral allegory has never been applied to "Where Are You Going. . . ." This brief study, however, seeks to elucidate "Where Are You Going . . ." as existential allegory. It seems evident that members of Connie's family embody much of the same resigned acceptance of "excluded alternatives" as do the characters in *A Garden*. Burwell argues that each of the major characters in *A Garden* realizes that he is "part of a drama whose outcome has largely been determined but remains unknown."[2] Thus, in refusing to attend a family picnic, Connie is rejecting not only her family's company, but the settled order of their existence—in which recognition of "excluded alternatives" is tantamount to acceptance of their lives.

The popular music which permeates "Where Are You Going . . ." is at the same time the narrative's *zeitgeist* and *leitmotiv*, serving as the former in order to maintain plausible realism, and the latter to establish allegorical significance. The recurring music then, while ostensibly innocuous realistic detail, is in fact, the vehicle of Connie's seduction and because of its intangibility, not immediately recognizable as such. Attesting to the significance of the *zeitgeist* in this narrative, "Where Are You Going . . ." is dedicated to Bob Dylan, who contributed to making music almost religious in dimension among the youth. It is music—instead of an apple—which lures Connie, quickens her heartbeat; and popular lyrics which constitute Friend's conversation and cadence—his promises, threats, and the careless confidence with which he seduces her.

Connie fuses unexplored sexuality with the mystery of the music when, at home, she thinks about her encounters: "But all the boys fell back and dissolved into a single face that was not even a face but an idea, a feeling, mixed up with the urgent insistent pounding of the music."

Before Friend arrives, Connie is bored and perhaps regrets not having gone to the cook-out with her family, so she goes in the house and turns on the radio "to drown out the quiet." Friend understands that music is sexual currency by pointing out his companion's radio when he invites her for a ride. And he succeeds in breaking her conversational ice by discussing the merits of a commonly admired singer.

Oates employs musical metaphor in her description of Friend. "He spoke in a simple lilting voice, exactly as if he were reciting the words to a song." Intrinsic to Friend's function is the fact that he himself is a record. While waiting for Connie to accept his ride offer, "he began to mark time with the music from Ellie's radio." Even their union is presaged by the sexually pointed observation of Connie listening "to the music from her radio and the boy's blend together."

The images which overtly suggest religious allegory while more subtly supporting the existential theme, are interspersed throughout the work. When Connie and her girl friend first enter the local "hang-out" where the girls and boys meet, they feel "as if they were entering a sacred building" where background music seems like that of a "church service." The day of the cook-out, which is significant both because it is the day of her defiance of her parents and the day of her capitulation to Friend, is a Sunday. "None of them bothered with church" identifies her spiritual vacuity. When Connie first hears Friend's car enter the driveway, she whispers "Christ," as later Friend evokes the name of Christ with a curse when she threatens to call the police.

Friend is a strange syncretism of O'Connor's Bible-peddling Manley Pointer in manner, and Satan in appearance. When Connie first observes Friend, she notices his "shaggy black hair," his "jalopy painted gold,"[3] and his broad grin. As the narrative progresses, his features appear more ominous, his hair like a wig, his slitted eyes "like chips of broken glass" with "thick black tarlike" lashes when not covered by mirrored, but masking sunglasses; and he looks older. Like Milton's Satan "crested aloft and Carbuncle his Eyes with burnished Neck of verdant Gold, erect,"[4] Friend posited atop his golden jalopy, has a muscular neck which suggests the reptilian, as does the fact that he "slid" rather than stepped out of the car. His feet resemble the devil's cloven hooves: "One of his boots was at a strange angle, as if his foot wasn't in it."

Friend's mesmeric influence on Connie further supports my contention that he represents a superhuman force. "Don't you know who I am?" he asks in an eery fashion, as if she had encountered him before, as one does evil. She is unable to make a telephone call for help because he is watching her; she bumps against a piece of furniture in a familiar room; and when he commands her to do what would otherwise seem an irrational act, to place her hand on her heart to understand its flaccidity, she readily obeys. His directives culminate when he convinces her, "What else is there for a girl like you but to be sweet and pretty and give in."

The recurring use of a twentieth-century symbol of irony—the false smile—further veils the existential meaning in realistic narrative. Over the student drive-in hangs a "revolving figure of a grinning boy holding a hamburger aloft." And Friend intersperses smiles with threats. "'Connie, don't fool around with me. I mean—I mean, don't fool *around*,' he said shaking his head. He laughed incredulously." Friend demands a smile from his conquest as well: "Now come out through the kitchen with me, honey, and let's see a smile."

In the end, Oates makes it clear that Connie, in capitulating to Friend, is not simply surrendering her virginal innocence, but bowing to absolute forces which her youthful coquetry cannot direct—absolute forces over which she has no control. At this point she thinks for the first time in her life that her heart "was nothing that was hers . . . but just a pounding, living thing inside this body that wasn't really hers either."

In the seduction which Friend engineers, Connie is merely the personification of the female he wishes to dominate, to be taller than, to despoil. The phrases he delivers from his musical repertoire are not even tailored to Connie: "'My sweet little blue-eyed girl' he said in a half-sung sigh that had nothing to do with her brown eyes."

In the presentation of this complex narrative, the major characters represent two distinct personifications in the dual levels of the allegory. It is apparent that Friend represents the devil who tempts the chaste yet morally vacuous girl-victim. Yet upon closer analysis, it appears that Connie takes the active part as *Everyman* experiencing the inevitable realization of her insignificance and powerlessness while Friend, who personifies the Erinyes, is merely the catalyst.

Although Oates uses the trappings of a realist to craft plausible characters—a dreamy teenaged girl, a hypnotic Manson-like man—and renders a facsimile of awkward adolescent behavior and speech, with contemporary youth's devotion to popular music as a convincing *zeitgeist,* this must not obscure her design. She presents an allegory which applies existential initiation rites to the Biblical seduction myth to represent *Everyman's* transition from the illusion of free will to the realization of externally determined fate.

☐ *Notes* ∎

1. Samuel F. Pickering, Jr., "The Short Stories of Joyce Carol Oates," *Georgia Review* 28 (1974), 218–226.

2. Rose Marie Burwell, "Joyce Carol Oates and an Old Master," *Critique: Studies in Modern Fiction* 15 (1973), 48–57.

3. This also seems to be a parody of the Cinderella tale. Painted on the golden car is a "drawing of a round, grinning face that reminded Connie of a pumpkin."

4. John Milton, *Paradise Lost,* IX, 500–501.

A Source For "Where Are You Going, Where Have You Been?"

One of Joyce Carol Oates's most familiar and most disturbing short stories—"Where Are You Going, Where Have You Been?"—is so richly symbolic and her characters are so improbably dressed and motivated that one is tempted to see it exclusively as a play of primal forces rather than as a fiction derived from and responsive to life itself. One critic, in fact, has argued that the story is an allegory.[1] And, indeed, the characters in the story seem larger than life. Her villains (and there is no mistaking that they are villains) are actuated by raw emotions, or none at all, outfitted in the most unlikely and sinister ways, and possessed of an unaccountable knowledge of the doings of the victim and her family. The victim herself is a freshly washed, blond, blue-eyed picture of innocence. But however attractive a view it may be to imagine Ms. Oates conceiving of a modern "tale" in the tradition of Hawthorne and Poe which freely mingles the marvelous with the psychologically true, it is contrary to the overwhelming evidence that the author drew her inspiration for her story from a real event publicized in popular national magazines. This view also injures the story itself for it diverts our attention from the fact that the evil she portrays is all too real and renders ineffective the pointed criticism Oates makes of the American Dream, which is the larger purpose of her story. Rather, Oates mod-

From *Studies in Short Fiction* 18 (1981): 413–420.

elled her story after real people and real events—though she did, as any gifted writer does, imaginatively transform the actual into a fiction of dramatic power. It is my purpose here, then, to identify the parallels between her story and the magazine reports of a real criminal and a real crime which seem to have had a germinal effect upon Oates's creative imagination and to suggest how her theme of the death of the American Dream may have been prompted by these magazines.

The source of and inspiration for Oates's fiend, Arnold Friend, is not nearly so mysterious as the almost supernatural attributes of this character might suggest. Oates's character, as I shall demonstrate, was derived from the exploits, widely publicized by *Time, Life,* and *Newsweek* magazines during the winter of 1965–66, of a real killer from Tucson, Arizona.[2] Moreover, the publication date of "Where Are You Going, Where Have You Been?" in *Epoch* (Fall 1966) suggests this influence, though the more accessible appearance of the story later in her collection of short stories, *The Wheel of Love* (1970), tends to obscure the implication that she probably wrote the story soon after her acquaintance with the grisly details of the three murders committed by a young man named Charles Howard Schmid and nick-named by the author of the *Life* piece about him as the "Pied Piper of Tucson."

Oddly enough, those very details which, by their peculiarity, tend to mark Arnold Friend as an inhuman, perhaps superhuman avatar of undiluted evil are derivative rather than invented. Charles Schmid, an extremely short and muscular man, was a mere five feet three inches tall but nevertheless had been a state champion in gymnastics during his high school years. After being suspended from high school for stealing tools from the auto shop, he continued to inhabit well beyond his teen years such high school haunts as drive-in restaurants, bowling alleys, and the public swimming pool. He was, in fact, twenty-three years old when he was arrested for the murders of Gretchen and Wendy Fritz, aged seventeen and thirteen, in the fall of 1965 and while an earlier third murder of Alleen Rowe, fifteen, was still being investigated. To compensate for his shortness and to disguise the fact that he was a good deal older than the teenaged girls to whom he was attracted, Schmid went to bizarre and rather stagey extremes.

As all the national magazines pointed out, Schmid stuffed rags and folded tin cans into his black leather boots to appear a few inches taller. And he dyed his hair raven black, often wore pancake make-up, pale cream lipstick, and mascara. He sometimes darkened his face to a "tan" with make-up and painted a beauty mark on his cheek.

His behavior was as audacious as his appearance. He drove a gold colored car, in which he "cruised" Tucson's Speedway Boulevard. And he was known to tell tall-tales about how he came into the money he habitually flourished—to his male admirers he suggested that he trafficked in drugs; to the females he bragged that he had been paid by women whom he had taught "a hundred ways to make love." He was also inclined to introduce himself by a number of aliases, his favorite being "Angel Rodriguez."

The parallels in "Where Are You Going?" to the reports of the Schmid case are too clear-cut to have been accidental. The young victim of Arnold Friend's attention, Connie, notices that he, like Schmid, is quite short: "He wasn't tall, only an inch or so taller than she would be if she came down to him." But he, like the gymnast Schmid, is muscular as well. He wore a "belt that pulled his waist in and showed how lean he was, and a white pull-over shirt that was a little soiled and showed the hard, small muscles of his arms and shoulders. He looked as if he probably did hard work, lifting and carrying things. Even his neck looked muscular." And Arnold Friend totters and wobbles on his black, leather boots and eventually almost loses his balance. This draws Connie's attention to his feet: "He had to bend and adjust his boots. Evidently his feet did not go all the way down; the boots must have been stuffed with something so that he would seem taller."

Oates's description of Friend's face was probably derived from the several photographs reprinted in national magazines. One photo in particular may have been influential for it showed Schmid, as Oates had described Friend, with "cheeks slightly darkened because he hadn't shaved for a day or two, and the nose long and hawklike." And Schmid's dark eyes in this photograph may well have impressed her as "chips of broken glass that catch the light in an amiable way." But more concretely, Friend also wears make-up, as did Schmid.

His eye lashes are extremely dark, "as if painted with a black tarlike material," and he may even be wearing a wig. Connie notes Friend's fascinating but dangerous smile, "as if he were smiling from inside a mask." "His whole face was a mask, she thought wildly, tanned down to his throat but then running out as if he had plastered make-up on his face but had forgotten about his throat."

In incidental ways, too, Arnold Friend recalls Charles Schmid. Friend also drives a gold car, apparently older than the gold car Schmid owned, but newly painted. He is older than the boys with whom Connie is familiar; though Oates makes his age a question, Connie thinks he may be thirty, even older. And Arnold Friend is characterized by the same sort of compensating braggadocio Schmid's friends remembered of him in the magazine articles: "He sounded like a hero in a movie, declaring something important. But he spoke too loudly and it was as if he were speaking to someone behind Connie." Moreover, the shocking and confident sexual directness of Friend contrasts sharply with the "caresses of love" Connie dreamed of before Friend pulled into her drive, "sweet, gentle, the way it was in the movies and promised in songs." Schmid's habitual brag to teenaged girls that he knew "one hundred ways to make love" is only slightly less direct than Friend's brag to Connie: "I'll hold you so tight you won't think you have to get away or pretend anything because you'll know you can't. And I'll come inside you where it's all secret and you'll give in to me, and you'll love me." "People don't talk like that," says Connie, but of course some people do, and Charles Schmid apparently did. Finally, even the name of Oates's villain may have been suggested by the *Life* article. For, whatever other symbolic suggestion the name may have, the irony of a young man who had once tied a string to the tail of his pet cat and had beaten it against the wall until it was a bloody mass but nevertheless assumed the alias "Angel" could hardly have been lost upon Oates's artistic sensibility. Surely she intended the same sort of irony in naming her demoniac character "Friend."

For the violent crime implied in "Where Are You Going?"—the rape and subsequent murder of Connie—which is not dramatized but is a sure eventuality, Oates also seems to

84

have drawn upon the story of Charles Schmid, but she made certain alterations in the details of it. Alleen Rowe was, like Connie, fifteen years old at the time of her assault, and she too had washed her hair just before her assailants arrived. Rowe's rape and murder also involved accomplices with an apparent knowledge of her parents' habits. Friend, it will be remembered, knows Connie's name, that her family is gone to a barbeque, and how long they will be gone. Arnold Friend is accompanied by Ellie, a rather passive if not oblivious accomplice to be sure, but Schmid's violent crime involved a young man, John Saunders, and a young woman, Mary French. Apparently on the spur of the moment, these three wondered whether they might kill someone and get away with it.[3] Because she had once "stood up" John Saunders, they decided upon Alleen Rowe and went to her house the same evening. Perhaps by a "fortunate" coincidence or perhaps aware that Alleen's mother worked nights, they found Alleen home alone. Mary French tapped on Alleen's window and eventually persuaded her to go for a drive with them. In the desert, the two men raped her and then beat her to death, and the three buried her in the sand.

The rape of the Rowe girl was, according to the *Newsweek* account of the murder, an afterthought. The *Newsweek* article is entitled "Killing for Kicks" and it portrays the real criminal act as very nearly motiveless and unaccountable. In fact, *Life, Time,* and *Newsweek* all preferred to lay the blame on a generation of indulgent, cruising teenagers and their unmindful parents. But Ms. Oates modified the details of the actual event in significant ways. For one thing, she has Connie's seduction conducted in broad daylight while her family is away at a family barbeque and has Arnold Friend display intimate, even satanic knowledge of her family's doings. Also, she chose to downplay Saunder's part in the murder and eliminated the role of Mary French altogether. It is Friend, rather than his accomplice, who is apparently offended by the casual snub he receives at a drive-in restaurant and says to Connie, "Gonna get you, baby." And she seems to have combined Schmid's reputation as a "pied piper" with Mary French's inducements to Alleen to leave her house in the character of Arnold Friend. Thus, she gave to her story an unsettling tension by locating the evil in a single character whose motive was even slighter than John Saunder's and who was not afraid to tempt her in the daytime.

Oates also seems to have combined Schmid's three victims into one, or perhaps two characters. The murder of Wendy Fritz had been the result of her having accompanied her older sister Gretchen to the desert with Schmid. Oates suggests at least the unintentional complicity of Connie's older sister June, whom Connie resents because her mother continually reminds Connie what a model daughter June is. But Connie's parents allow her to go out at night with her friends because June does the same; and it is this freedom that brings Connie into the orbit of Arnold Friend. But Connie also resembles Alleen Rowe in her age, her freshly washed hair, her love for rock and roll music, and, as *Life* described it, a susceptible, romantic mentality.

Thus far our discussion of Oates's reaction to an actual incident has focused upon the particular ways she took suggestions from the documented reports of Schmid's violent crimes and dramatized them in her story. But, more significantly, she seems also to have taken her cues from these magazine reports in more general ways which may account for the related thematic elements of seductive rock and roll and violently extinguished innocence which permeate her story.

One cannot help but pause and ponder Oates's dedication of this story to Bob Dylan. However, it is a mistake, I think, to conclude with Urbanski that the dedication is pejorative because Dylan made music "almost religious in dimension among youth." Rather, it is honorific because the history and effect of Bob Dylan's music had been to draw youth away from the romantic promises and frantic strains of a brand of music sung by Buddy Holly, Chuck Berry, Elvis Presley and others. It was Bob Dylan, after all, who told us that the "times they are a changin'," and one of Oates's aims in her short story is to show that they have already changed. It is the gyrating, hip-grinding music of people like Elvis Presley, whom Schmid identified as his "idol," which emanates from Ellie's transistor radio, the "hard, fast, shrieking" songs played by the disk jockey "Bobby King" rather than the cryptic, atonal folk music of Bob Dylan.

Both Connie and Arnold Friend are enthusiastic about "Bobby King" and psychologically linked to one another by an appreciation of the rhythmic beat of the music he plays. Connie observes that Ellie's radio is tuned to the same station as her radio in the house, and when Arnold Friend says that King is "great," Connie concedes, "He's kind of great." Arnold counters, "Listen, that guy is *great*. He knows where the action is." Friend's statement of enthusiasm recalls the quotation that introduces the *Life* essay on Charles Schmid:

> "Hey, c'mon babe, follow me,
> I'm the Pied Piper, follow me,
> I'm the Pied Piper
> And I'll show you where it's at.
> —Popular song,
> Tucson, winter 1965

Arnold Friend does, indeed, show Connie "where it's at," and he draws her from the house with his alternating blandishments and threats much as a pied piper. Moreover, Connie's ultimate, mindless decision to go with Friend is meant to recall the beckoning tempo of rock and roll: "She cried out, she cried for her mother, she felt her breath start jerking back and forth in her lungs as if it were something Arnold Friend was stabbing her with again and again with no tenderness. A noisy, sorrowful wailing rose all about her and she was locked inside the way she was locked inside the house."

When Connie kicks the telephone away and opens the screen door to go with Friend, there can be little question where she is going nor where she has been. She is going to her death, and her fate is largely the result of a consciousness shaped by the frantic life of cruising in fast cars, sipping cokes out of sweating paper cups with anonymous boys, a consciousness epitomized by the frantic music she listens to.

But it is naive to suppose that this story is about the dangerous effects of rock and roll; rather, the music is emblematic of the tempo of American life generally. And the question in the title—where are you going, where have you been?—are addressed to America itself. The author of the *Life* article asked sarcastically, "Isn't Tucson—out there in the Golden West, in the grand setting where the skies are not cloudy all day—supposed to be a flowering of the American Dream? Oates's short story is her withering, disturbing reply, and her story is very nearly a suspenseful parody of the mythic promises of the West and "Home on the Range." For Connie's house is distant from any others and the "encouraging words" Arnold Friend speaks are hypnotic enough to lure her out of doors beneath a perfectly blue, cloudless sky.

Insofar as this story has a setting, it is set in the West. Connie's parents leave for a family "barbeque," and their daughter daydreams in the summer heat ("It was too hot," she thinks), under the sky "perfectly blue and still." She stares from her "asbestos 'ranch house'" to the limitless expanse of land outside it. Her house seems small to her, and Arnold reminds her that the walls of her house do not provide a citadel: "The place where you came from ain't there any more, and where you had in mind to go is cancelled out. This place you are now—inside your daddy's house—is nothing but a cardboard box I can knock down any time. You know that and always did know it. You hear me?" Her "asbestos" house is no protection from the devilish forces embodied in Arnold Friend, nor from his fiery passion and never has been. If there were a fire inside, Friend tells her, "If the place got lit up with a fire, honey, you'd come runnin' out into my arms an' safe at home."

Of course there is a fire inside, a fire inside Connie's brain. The pounding of her heart is simply "a pounding, living thing inside this body that really wasn't really her either." Arnold's "incantation" draws her out, but those values generally associated with the American Dream, of hearth and home and innocent youth, are by this time a dim flicker in her mind. Thoughts of "Aunt Tillie's" barbeque, hot dogs and corn on the cob, tender flirtations, the lovely promises of songs are now remote, almost as though they had never been. As she steps out to Arnold Friend, she sees the land: "the vast sunlit reaches of the land behind him and on all sides of him—so much land that Connie had never seen before and did not recognize except to know that she was going to it." When one knows that Charles Schmid buried his victims in the desert, the dictum of the American Dream that one ought to return to the land, that nature speaks to us in lasting and benevolent ways, takes on a singularly sinister connotation. The American Dream is quite extinct here, and Connie's parents and sister are as much dreamers as she. Ultimately, the questions which Oates chose as a title for her story might be asked about America itself as well as about Connie's life, and asked more effectively in the slang idiom of Connie's generation: "Where *are you* going? Where *have you* been?" For they address a society which, by tradition, has preferred its agrarian dreams and promises to harsher realities and aggressive evils and is therefore dangerously blind to them. Our antique values, says Oates, are not proof against the seductions of the piper's song.

☐ *Notes* ■

1. Marie Mitchell Olesen Urbanski, "Existential Allegory: Joyce Carol Oates's 'Where Are You Going, Where Have You Been?'" Reprinted in this volume.

2. "Secrets in the Sand," *Time,* 26 November 1965, p. 28; Dan Moser, "The Pied Piper of Tucson," *Life,* 4 March 1966, (reprinted in this volume); "Growing Up in Tucson: Death of Sentence," *Time,* 11 March 1966, p. 28; and "Killing for Kicks" *Newsweek,* 14 March 1966, pp. 35–36.

Since some of the parallels between the Oates short story and the national magazine coverage of the Charles Schmid case occur only in the *Life* essay—for example, the fact that the real victim, Alleen Rowe, and Oates's fictional victim, Connie, both washed their hair shortly before the arrival of their assailant—it seems likely that this essay was the primary, if not the sole source of Oates's familiarity with the story. Therefore, all the information about the murder case has been taken from the *Life* piece unless otherwise indicated in the text or by footnote.

3. "Killing for Kicks," *Newsweek,* 14 March 1966, pp. 35–36.

☐ JOAN D. WINSLOW ■

The Stranger Within:
Two Stories by
Oates and Hawthorne

In her story "Where Are You Going, Where Have You Been?",
Joyce Carol Oates describes her main character, Connie, in
this way: "She wore a pullover jersey blouse that looked one
way when she was at home and another way when she was
away from home. Everything about her had two sides to it, one
for home and one for anywhere that was not home." This detail tells us that Connie's identity is split: one part of her displays her emerging sexuality; the other part conforms to what
the authorities in her life consider proper. Many of Oates's
characters have this two-sided quality: one side ordinary and
respectable, the other side ruled by such forbidden impulses
as lust, violence, and hate. Often in her stories this under-side
of the human personality erupts and compels these characters toward obsessive love affairs, cruelty, brutality, and even
murder.

Yet society, and its representation in the individual con-
science, persistently try to ignore or deny these underground
emotions that can lead to sin and crime. To Oates, such refusal to acknowledge that these feelings are a part of human
existence is a greater evil than the expression of the forbidden
impulses. In *Expensive People*, Richard's furious tantrum in
the flower bed is deliberately misunderstood and made to
seem "quite all right"; nevertheless, his ignored anger grows

From *Studies in Short Fiction* 17 (1980): 262–268.

until it ends in a (real or delusionary) murder. The denial of human emotions, however unpleasant or frightening they may be, is far more dangerous than the emotions themselves.

This concern with the human tendency to deny the evil inherent in human nature also informs the fiction of an earlier American writer, Nathaniel Hawthorne. It is my contention that these two writers conceive of human personality similarly, and that both show the need to accept its coloring of evil. When Hawthorne's Aylmer is compelled to erase the one blemish on his bride's perfection, the birthmark on her cheek, he causes her death; deprived of this imperfection, she can no longer exist as a human being. The minister Dimmesdale, like Connie, finds it necessary to split his identity: to outward eyes he is the perfect spiritual leader, but underneath his clerical garments the sign of his sin is embedded on his breast.

The respectable, daylight side of human personality differs in the two writers, for the cultures they write about are very different. Hawthorne's community has strong traditions and a vital religion, while Oates's characters live in a society valuing money and social status and define themselves according to media images. The dark side of human nature, though, is very much alike for the two writers: it is comprised of the impulses of sexual passion, violence, cruelty, and hate. Samuel F. Pickering, Jr., writing on Oates, terms these impulses "demons . . . rising from suppressed psychological urges within."[1] Pickering is speaking metaphorically, but in Oates's story "Where Are You Going, Where Have You Been?", a demon or devil figure does literally confront the protagonist. Hawthorne's fiction too uses this archetypal figure, traditionally a symbol for the "evil" tendencies within human beings, notably in "Young Goodman Brown." The convention of an encounter with the devil—really an encounter with a part of oneself—is especially revealing because once a character has projected his emotions outside himself, his attitude toward this subterranean self can be made much more concrete. This discussion will focus on these two tales of an encounter with the devil. They are strikingly similar in structure and meaning. The use of a traditional narrative pattern brings these two writers from different centuries, writing about very different cultures, much closer together and makes the resemblances in their visions easier to see.

In "Where Are You Going, Where Have You Been?", the fifteen-year-old protagonist, Connie, chooses to stay at home one Sunday while her parents and older sister go off to a family barbecue. As she is listening to the radio, a gold-painted jalopy drives into the yard with two occupants, a boy Connie has seen once before, who identifies himself as Arnold Friend, and his companion Ellie, who listens to a transistor radio all during the conversation between Arnold and Connie. Arnold invites Connie to go for a ride with him, but she feigns disinterest, uncertain whether she wants to go. As their dialogue progresses, Connie begins to see that Arnold is not what he appears to be: his hair, face, clothes, and talk are all a disguise. As her fear grows, Arnold becomes more and more insistent that she go with him and gradually reveals his power over her. At the end the terrified girl finds herself moving irresistibly toward him and the "vast sunlit" land behind him.

In "Young Goodman Brown," Brown leaves his wife one evening in order to meet a stranger in the forest, apparently to go with him to a witch-meeting. During their conversation Brown's reluctance to proceed onward is gradually overcome by the stranger's assertions and demonstrations that those people Brown has always believed virtuous are journeying toward the meeting in the forest. As Brown is about to be formally initiated into the fellowship of evil, along with his wife whom he finds there, he cries out to her to resist, and all signs of the assembly vanish. Brown returns home to a life of suspicion and gloom, and Hawthorne raises the question of whether the meeting was only a dream.

Although Connie and Goodman Brown at first seem utterly dissimilar characters, an examination of their lives and thoughts at the time of the encounters with these two devil figures reveals a number of meaningful resemblances suggesting that the writers' views of human personality are close. The most significant similarity seems to be the connection with a sexual initiation. The figures appear to the two protagonists at a time in their lives when both are entering into sexual experience. Brown is "three months married," and the marriage, we assume, has discovered in him a sexual passion he had been unaware of before and is having difficulty accepting. Although Hawthorne does not make the sexual level of his story explicit, it has regularly been interpreted in this way. The discovery of sin in the adults of the community whom Brown has always thought virtuous, the loss of respect for his father and grandfather through learning of their involvement with the figure of evil, the fact that Brown and his wife are to be initiated as a couple into this society and will then know of the sin in all other adults, and the phallic suggestions in the description of the setting of this ceremony—all give support to this interpretation. Brown's new participation in sex and his new awareness of his own sexual desire are moving him across the threshold between innocence and knowledge, childhood and adulthood, but this is a movement about which he feels guilty and fearful.

Connie, if we are to take as true Arnold's statement, "You don't know what that is but you will," has not yet experienced sexual intercourse, but she is moving toward it. She spends hours parked in dark alleys with boys she meets. So far these tentative experiments with sex seem to her "sweet, gentle, the way it was in movies and promised in songs." But she is conscious of another attitude about sex, which she rejects: "the way someone like June [her older sister] would suppose." These repressed negative feelings of revulsion, fear, and guilt appear to Connie in the projected figure of Arnold Friend. For Arnold proposes to become her lover and to initiate her fully into sexuality. Connie reacts to this articulation of where she is headed with terror: "'Shut up! You're crazy!' . . . She backed away from the door. She put her hands against her ears as if she'd heard something terrible, something not meant for her." Her feelings cause her to associate Arnold with danger, nightmare, and death, just as Brown's guilt entangles sex with evil and loss of faith in virtuousness. Connie is moving tentatively toward an experience she—like Brown—will be unable to handle emotionally. Neither protagonist is able to accept the full reality of his/her sexual nature, but instead turns it into something evil and frightening and projects it into the form of a devil.

There are many parallels in the structure of the en-

94

counter with the devil in the two stories. For both protagonists, their involvement requires the deception of another person, someone close to them who is concerned about their welfare and who represents the values of society. Both deceive this person as to the truth of their moral and emotional situations and by doing so refuse help in their moral danger. Brown's wife Faith feels strangely anxious over his journey and asks him to stay with her that night. Brown's jocular answer, "What . . . dost thou doubt me already?" is a response which rejects Faith's concern and forces her to accept his departure. Immediately afterward, Brown acknowledges to himself his falseness: "What a wretch am I," and the moral distance he is placing between himself and his wife: "'t would kill her to think it." In Connie's case it is her mother, who, occasionally feeling a misgiving about her daughter's activities, asks at one point, "What's this about the Pettinger girl?" Connie's response, "Oh, her. That dope," deceptively separates herself from a girl we later discover is one of her close friends. Like Brown, she feels regret at this deception: "Her mother was so simple, Connie thought, that it was maybe cruel to fool her so much." By offering false reassurances, both protagonists cover up their true involvement and reject the help of someone who might guide or save them.

In a physical sense, too, both separate themselves from all ties in order to meet with the devil figures. Brown insists he must go on his errand despite Faith's anxiety, and Connie refuses to join her family's outing despite her mother's anger. Thus they isolate themselves from family and community. This isolation is both a necessary condition for the meeting with the devil and a result of previous involvement with evil, for they feel they cannot share this experience with their families. Because they already feel guilty, they cannot permit the openness that might save them.

Both characters seem to have made a preliminary commitment to the encounter. Brown has "kept covenant" in meeting the stranger in the forest. Connie's commitment is less conscious; it seems to have occurred at the moment Arnold first saw her, when, having just been picked up by Eddie, her face was "gleaming" with joy and pleasure. Although Connie believes she has made no engagement with Arnold, he insists that she is expecting him. Despite the commitment, though, when actually confronted with the strangers, both become doubtful and afraid. The ambivalence of their responses can be seen in the uncertain physical movements each displays. Connie hesitates, half inside and half outside the screen door, refusing to go with Arnold but not fully withdrawing herself either. Brown vacillates between a refusal to continue on and an almost unconscious progress deeper into the forest.

The devil figures themselves have both similarities and differences. They are semi-strangers, familiar and yet unknown. Both have supernatural powers and a remarkable knowledge of their victims' lives. They display various characteristics traditionally associated with the devil. Connie's devil is more clearly sexual, taking a form like that of her boyfriends and proposing to become her lover. The numbers of the "secret code" painted on his car also carry a sexual meaning, for they add up to 69. He is linked with death as well: his threats suggest more and more definitely that Connie is to die, and at one point he seems to be trying to reassure her by mentioning a neighbor who has died: "Don't you like her?" The inadequacy of his disguise—the slang just a little out of date, the makeup that covers his face but not his neck, the voice that suddenly sounds just like the announcer on the radio—these details are both comic and sinister, as is his name, Arnold Friend. The knowing reader can easily identify him as the devil, although it is uncertain whether Connie does; for example, his awkwardness in walking suggests to her that his boots are stuffed with something so that he will seem taller, but our imaginations penetrate further and recognize the cloven feet of the devil.

Brown's devil is more companion than antagonist, although he is that, too. He awakens and affirms Brown's doubt of others and his belief that he is irrevocably committed to evil. Much more than Brown, Connie is surprised at the manifestation of her devil. This difference reflects the degree of consciousness each character has of the guilt within him/her. Connie has repressed any doubt, transforming her feelings into the clichés of songs and movies, and is astonished at the consequences of her behavior. She belongs to the line of Oates characters who are overwhelmed by the discovery of the dark

96

instincts within them; Arnold turns out to be more powerful and frightening than she could have expected. Brown, on the other hand, has been struggling with his doubts and feelings of sinfulness more consciously, and therefore is not so alarmed at their materialization in the form of a mysterious stranger.

The endings of the stories are quite different; that is because Oates's story ends at the crisis point whereas Hawthorne's continues beyond it to show the way Brown is affected by his experience in his later life. Once we see that it is the different ending points that make the stories seem to end so differently, similarities in the experiences become more apparent. Possibly, we are meant to understand that Connie dies at the end of her story. But if we do not take the death suggestions literally, they communicate a meaning something like the ending of "Young Goodman Brown": just as a part of Brown, his trust in the goodness of others, dies, so a part of Connie dies, perhaps her innocence or her ignorance of the darker side of sexual passion.

The stories share a dream-like atmosphere and make the suggestion that each protagonist's experience was a dream. Hawthorne raises the question explicitly: "Had Goodman Brown fallen asleep in the forest and only dreamed a wild dream of a witch-meeting?" Oates hints at a similar explanation: Connie had fallen asleep once outside in the sun; she is sitting on her bed "bathed in a glow of slow-pulsed joy" emanating from the music on her radio when she hears the car outside. The question of whether the encounter was dream or reality permits two levels of interpretation for the stories: each can be read as a fantasy about a supernatural encounter and as a psychological analysis of the emotional state which could create such a dream.

The similarities in narrative pattern pointed out here, I believe, reflect a similar theme. Both Connie and Goodman Brown encounter their devils because they have tried to avoid a recognition of the disturbing character of human nature. Connie's experiences with sex must arouse in her feelings of confusion and uneasiness, but she forces her real feelings to fit the stereotypes imposed by songs and movies. She is determined to maintain in her own mind her superiority to the judgment of her mother and sister. Yet the effort to force her experience to fit a false shape becomes too difficult, and her repressed fear, uncertainty, and guilt finally emerge in the shape of Arnold Friend.

Brown holds to an even stricter framework into which he fits his experience of the world: people are either completely virtuous or completely evil. Even the discovery in himself of what he considers sin does not destroy the framework he has erected, for instead of acknowledging that good and evil exist in all people, he merely shifts all those he thought virtuous into the evil category. He resists the allegorical lesson shown him at the meeting when he sees "grave, reputable, and pious people" "consorting" with "men of dissolute lives and women of spotted fame." His reaction reveals the strength of his categories: "It was strange to see that the good shrank not from the wicked, nor were the sinners abashed by the saints." Just as he cannot accept the mingling of these people at the meeting, so he does not accept the lesson of his experience: that human nature is a mixture of good and evil impulses.

Both stories show that when we hide the knowledge of these disturbing impulses from ourselves, their inevitable emergence—whether as devil figure or unexpected aberrant behavior—surprises and terrifies us. If these two encounters with the devil were intended to force the protagonists to move from two-sidedness into a full awareness of themselves, neither seems to succeed. However, by means of their stories Oates and Hawthorne are urging their readers to break free of such categorizing and recognize that violence, lust, hate and cruelty are a part of human nature.

☐ Notes ∎

1. Samuel F. Pickering, Jr., "The Short Stories of Joyce Carol Oates," *Georgia Review* 28 (1974), 221.

JOYCE M. WEGS ■

"Don't You Know Who I Am?" The Grotesque in Oates's "Where Are You Going, Where Have You Been?"

Joyce Carol Oates's ability to absorb and then to transmit in her fiction the terror which is often a part of living in America today has been frequently noted and admired. For instance, Walter Sullivan praises her skill by noting that "horror resides in the transformation of what we know best, the intimate and comfortable details of our lives made suddenly threatening."[1] Although he does not identify it as such, Sullivan's comment aptly describes a classic instance of a grotesque intrusion: a familiar world suddenly appears alien. Oates frequently evokes the grotesque in her fiction, drawing upon both its traditional or demoniac and its contemporary or psychological manifestations.[2] In the prize-winning short story, "Where Are You Going, Where Have You Been?", Oates utilizes the grotesque in many of its forms to achieve a highly skillful integration of the multiple levels of the story and, in so doing, to suggest a transcendent reality which reaches beyond surface realism to evoke the simultaneous mystery and reality of the contradictions of the human heart. Full of puzzling and perverse longings, the heart persists in mixing lust and love, life and death, good and evil. Oates's teenage protagonist, Connie, discovers that her dream love-god also wears the face of lust, evil, and death.

From *Journal of Narrative Technique* 5 (1975): 66–72.

Centering the narrative on the world of popular teenage music and culture, Oates depicts the tawdry world of drive-in restaurants and shopping plazas blaring with music with a careful eye for authentic surface detail. However, her use of popular music as a thematic referent is typical also of her frequent illumination of the illusions and grotesquely false values which may arise from excessive devotion to such aspects of popular culture as rock music, movies, and romance magazines. In all of her fiction as in this story, she frequently employs a debased religious imagery to suggest the gods which modern society has substituted for conventional religion. Oates delineates the moral poverty of Connie, her fifteen-year-old protagonist, by imaging a typical evening Connie spends at a drive-in restaurant as a grotesquely parodied religious pilgrimage. Left by her friend's father to stroll at the shopping center or go to a movie, Connie and her girlfriend immediately cross the highway to the restaurant frequented by older teenagers. A grotesque parody of a church, the building is bottle-shaped and has a grinning boy holding a hamburger aloft on top of it. Unconscious of any ludicrousness, Connie and her friend enter it as if going into a "sacred building" which will give them "what haven and blessing they yearned for." It is the music which is "always in the background, like music at a church service" that has invested this "bright-lit, fly-infested" place with such significance. Indeed, throughout the story the music is given an almost mythical character, for it evokes in Connie a mysterious pleasure, a "glow of slow-pulsed joy that seemed to rise mysteriously out of the music itself."

Although the story undoubtedly has a moral dimension, Oates does not take a judgmental attitude toward Connie.[3] In fact, much of the terror of the story comes from the recognition that there must be thousands of Connies. By carefully including telltale phrases, Oates demonstrates in an understated fashion why Connies exist. Connie's parents, who seem quite typical, have disqualified themselves as moral guides for her. At first reading, the reader may believe Connie's mother to be concerned about her daughter's habits, views, and friends; but basically their arguments are little more than a "pretense of exasperation, a sense that they . . . [are] tugging and struggling over something of little value to either of them." Connie herself is uncertain of her mother's motives for constantly picking at her; she alternates between a view that her mother's harping proceeds from jealousy of Connie's good looks now that her own have faded and a feeling that her mother really prefers her over her plain older sister June because she is prettier. In other words, to Connie and her mother, real value lies in beauty. Connie's father plays a small role in her life, but by paralleling repeated phrases, Oates suggests that this is precisely the problem. Because he does not "bother talking much" to his family, he can hardly ask the crucial parental questions, "Where are you going?" or "Where have you been?" The moral indifference of the entire adult society is underscored by Oates's parallel description of the father of Connie's friend, who also "never . . . [bothers] to ask" what they did when he picks up the pair at the end of one of their evenings out. Similarly, on Sunday morning, "none of them bothered with church," not even that supposed paragon, June.

Since her elders do not bother about her, Connie is left defenseless against the temptations represented by Arnold Friend. A repeated key phrase emphasizes her helplessness. As she walks through the parking lot of the restaurant with Eddie, she can not "help but" look about happily, full of joy in a life characterized by casual pickups and constant music. When she sees Arnold in a nearby car, she looks away, but her instinctive flirtatiousness triumphs and she can not "help but" look back. Later, like Lot's wife leaving Sodom and Gomorrah, she cannot "help but look back" at the plaza and drive-in as her friend's father drives them home. In Connie's case, the consequences of the actions she can not seem to help are less biblically swift to occur and can not be simply labeled divine retribution.

Since music is Connie's religion, its values are hers also. Oates does not include the lyrics to any popular songs here, for any observer of contemporary America could surely discern the obvious link between Connie's high esteem for romantic love and youthful beauty and the lyrics of scores of hit tunes. The superficiality of Connie's values becomes terrifyingly apparent when Arnold Friend, the external embodiment of the teenage ideal celebrated in popular songs, appears at

101

Connie's home in the country one Sunday afternoon when she is home alone, listening to music and drying her hair. It is no accident that Arnold's clothes, car, speech, and taste in music reflect current teenage chic almost exactly, for they constitute part of a careful disguise intended to reflect Arnold's self-image as an accomplished youthful lover.

Suspense mounts in the story as the reader realizes along with Connie that Arnold is not a teenager and is really thirty or more. Each part of his disguise is gradually revealed to be grotesquely distorted in some way. His shaggy black hair, "crazy as a wig," is evidently really a wig. The mask-like appearance of his face has been created by applying a thick coat of makeup; however, he has carelessly omitted his throat. Even his eyelashes appear to be made-up, but with some tar-like material. In his clothing, his disguise appears more successful, for Connie approves of the way he dresses, as "all of them dressed," in tight jeans, boots, and pullover. When he walks, however, Connie realizes that the runty Arnold, conscious that the ideal teenager dream lover is tall, has stuffed his boots; the result is, however, that he can hardly walk and staggers ludicrously. Attempting to bow, he almost falls. Similarly, the gold jalopy covered with teenage slang phrases seems authentic until Connie notices that one of them is no longer in vogue. Even his speech is not his own, for it recalls lines borrowed from disk jockeys, teenage slang, and lines from popular songs. Arnold's strange companion, Ellie Oscar, is just as grotesque as Arnold. Almost totally absorbed in listening to music and interrupting this activity only to offer threatening assistance to Arnold, Ellie is no youth either; he has the "face of a forty-year-old baby." Although Arnold has worked out his disguise with great care, he soon loses all subtlety in letting Connie know of his evil intentions; he is not simply crazy but a criminal with plans to rape and probably to murder Connie.

However, Arnold is far more than a grotesque portrait of a psychopathic killer masquerading as a teenager; he also has all the traditional sinister traits of that arch-deceiver and source of grotesque terror, the devil. As is usual with Satan, he is in disguise; the distortions in his appearance and behavior suggest not only that his identity is faked but also hint at

102

his real self. Equating Arnold and Satan is not simply a gratuitous connection designed to exploit traditional demonic terror, for the early pages of the story explicitly prepare for this linking by portraying popular music and its values as Connie's perverted version of religion. When Arnold comes up the drive, her first glance makes Connie believe that a teenage boy with his jalopy, the central figure of her religion, has arrived; therefore, she murmurs "Christ, Christ" as she wonders about how her newly-washed hair looks. When the car—a parodied golden chariot?—stops, a horn sounds "as if this were a signal Connie knew." On one level, the horn honks to announce the "second coming" of Arnold, a demonic Day of Judgment. Although Connie never specifically recognizes Arnold as Satan, her first comment to him both hints at his infernal origins and faithfully reproduces teenage idiom: "Who the *hell* do you think you are?" (emphasis mine) When he introduces himself, his name too hints at his identity, for "friend" is uncomfortably close to "fiend"; his initials could well stand for Arch Fiend. The frightened Connie sees Arnold as "only half real:" he "had driven up her driveway all right but had come from nowhere before that and belonged nowhere." Especially supernatural is his mysterious knowledge about her, her family, and her friends. At one point, he even seems to be able to see all the way to the barbecue which Connie's family is attending and to get a clear vision of what all the guests are doing. Typical of his ambiguous roles is his hint that he had something to do with the death of the old woman who lived down the road. It is never clear whether Arnold has killed her, has simply heard of her death, or knows about it in his devil role of having come to take her away to hell. Although Arnold has come to take Connie away, in his traditional role as evil spirit, he may not cross a threshold uninvited; he repeatedly mentions that he is not going to come in after Connie, and he never does. Instead, he lures Connie out to him. Part of his success may be attributed to his black magic in having put his sign on her—X for victim. Because the devil is not a mortal being, existing as he does in all ages, it is not surprising that he slips in remembering what slang terms are in vogue. Similarly, his foolish attempt at a bow may result from a mixup in temporal concepts of the ideal lover. In addition, his clumsy bow may be due to the fact that it must be difficult to manipulate boots if one has cloven feet!

Although Oates attempts to explain the existence of Connie, she makes no similar effort to explain the existence of Arnold, for that would constitute an answer to the timeless and insoluble problem of evil in the world. As this story shows, Oates would agree with Pope Paul VI's recent commentary on the "terrible reality" of evil in the world, but she would not, I feel sure, endorse his view of this evil as being literally embodied in a specific being. Pope Paul describes evil as "not merely a lack of something, but an effective agent, a living spiritual being, perverted and perverting. A terrible reality. Mysterious and frightening."[4] Oates's description of her own views on religion is in terms strikingly similar to the language used by Pope Paul. To her, religion is a "kind of psychological manifestation of deep powers, deep imaginative, mysterious powers, which are always with us, and what has in the past been called supernatural. I would prefer simply to call natural. However, though these things are natural, they are still inaccessible and cannot be understood, cannot be controlled."[5] Thus, although Arnold is clearly a symbolic Satan, he also functions on a psychological level.

On this level, Arnold Friend is the incarnation of Connie's unconscious erotic desires and dreams, but in uncontrollable nightmare form. When she first sees Arnold in the drive-in, she instinctively senses his sinister attraction, for she can not "help glancing back" at him. Her "trashy daydreams" are largely filled with blurred recollections of the caresses of the many boys she has dated. That her dreams are a kind of generalized sexual desire—although Connie does not consciously identify them as such—is made evident by Oates's description of Connie's summer dreams: "But all the boys fell back and dissolved into a single face that was not even a face but an idea, a feeling, mixed up with the urgent insistent pounding of the music and the humid night air of July." What is frightening about Arnold is that he voices and makes explicit her own sexual desires; teenage boys more usually project their similar message with "that sleepy dreamy smile that all the boys used to get across ideas they didn't want to put into words." Connie's reaction to his bluntness is one of horror: "People don't talk like that, you're crazy."

Connie's fear drives her into a grotesque separation of mind from body in which her unconscious self takes over and betrays her. Terror-stricken, she cannot even make her weak fingers dial the police; she can only scream into the phone. In the same way that she is Arnold's prisoner, locked inside the house he alternately threatens to knock down or burn down, she is also a prisoner of her own body: "A noisy sorrowful wailing rose all about her and she was locked inside it the way she was locked inside this house." Finally, her conscious mind rejects any connection with her body and its impulses; her heart seems "nothing that was hers" "but just a pounding, living thing inside this body that wasn't really hers either." In a sense, her body with its puzzling desires "decides" to go with Arnold although her rational self is terrified of him: "She watched herself push the door slowly open as if she were back safe somewhere in the other doorway, watching this body and this head of long hair moving out into the sunlight where Arnold Friend waited."

Oates encourages the reader to look for multiple levels in this story and to consider Arnold and Connie at more than face value by her repeated emphasis on the question of identity. The opening of the story introduces the concept to which both Connie and her mother seem to subscribe—being pretty means being someone. In fact, her mother's acid questions as she sees Connie at her favorite activity of mirror-gazing— "Who are you? You think you're so pretty?"—also introduce the converse of this idea, namely, that those who lack physical beauty have no identity. As does almost everything in the story, everything about Connie has "two sides to it." However, Connie's nature, one for at home and one for "anywhere that was not home," is simple in comparison to that of Arnold. Connie's puzzled questions at first query what role Arnold thinks he is playing: "Who the hell do you think you are?" Then she realizes that he sees himself all too literally as the man of her dreams, and she becomes more concerned about knowing his real identity. By the time that Arnold asks, "Don't you know who I am?" Connie realizes that it is no longer a simple question of whether he is a "jerk" or someone worth her attention but of just how crazy he is. By the end she knows him to be a murderer, for she realizes that she will never see her family again. However, only the reader sees Arnold's Satan identity. Connie's gradual realization of Arnold's identity brings with it a recognition of the actual significance of physical beauty: Arnold is indeed someone to be concerned about, even if he is no handsome youth. At the conclusion, Connie has lost all identity except that of victim, for Arnold's half-sung sigh about her blue eyes ignores the reality of her brown ones. In Arnold's view, Connie's personal identity is totally unimportant.

Dedicated to contemporary balladeer Bob Dylan, this story in a sense represents Oates's updated prose version of a ballad in which a demon lover carries away his helpless victim. By adding modern psychological insights, she succeeds in revealing the complex nature of the victim of a grotesque intrusion by an alien force; on one level, the victim actually welcomes and invites this demonic visitation. Like Bob Dylan, she grafts onto the ballad tradition a moral commentary which explores but does not solve the problems of the evils of our contemporary society; an analogous Dylan ballad is his "It's a Hard Rain's a Gonna' Fall." Even the title records not only the ritual parental questions but also suggests that there is a moral connection between the two questions: where Connie goes is related to where she has been. Oates does not judge Connie in making this link, however; Connie is clearly not in complete control over where she has been. The forces of her society, her family, and her self combine to make her fate inescapable.

☐ Notes ■

1. Walter Sullivan, "The Artificial Demon: Joyce Carol Oates and the Dimensions of the Real," *The Hollins Critic* 9, No. 4 (December 1972), 2.

2. Joyce Markert Wegs, "The Grotesque in Some American Novels of the Nineteen-Sixties: Ken Kesey, Joyce Carol Oates, Sylvia Plath," Diss., University of Illinois, 1973.

3. See Walter Sullivan,"Where Have All the Flowers Gone?:

The Short Story in Search of Itself," *Sewanee Review* 78, No. 3 (Summer 1970), 537.

4. Andrew M. Greeley, "The Devil, You Say," *The New York Times Magazine,* 4 Feb. 1973, p. 26, quotes an address by Pope Paul on 15 Nov. 1972, as reported in the Vatican newspaper.

5. Linda Kuehl, "An Interview with Joyce Carol Oates," *Commonweal* 91 (5 Dec. 1969), 308.

LARRY RUBIN ■

Oates's "Where Are You Going, Where Have You Been?"

In a recent essay Joyce M. Wegs brilliantly establishes the satanic identity of the sinister Arnold Friend, young Connie's abductor and probable rapist-murderer in Joyce Carol Oates's widely anthologized short story "Where Are You Going, Where Have You Been?"[1] On another level, the psychological level, she points out that Arnold is "the incarnation of Connie's unconscious erotic desires and dreams, but in uncontrollable nightmare form." I would go a step further and suggest that, on still another level, the whole terrifying episode involving Arnold Friend is itself a dream—a fantasy that Connie falls into on a sleepy Sunday afternoon when she is left alone in the house and decides to spend the entire day drying her hair.[2] For those of her readers who don't believe in devils, Oates has made the willing suspension of disbelief somewhat easier by imparting to her story a dreamlike, unreal atmosphere that makes it possible for the reader to view Connie's scary encounter with Arnold as a dream-vision or "daymare"—one in which Connie's intense desire for total sexual experience runs headlong into her innate fear of such experience.[3] We must remember that Connie is only fifteen; and the collision is gorgeous.

First of all, for all the talk of sex and boys in the story, we have no clear evidence that Connie is not still a virgin.

From *Explicator* 42 (1984): 57–59.

Sophisticated, yes—but only in the most superficial ways, involving the heightening of her physical charms. Even the brief time Connie spends with a boy named Eddie in an alley seems, in context, more in keeping with smooching or even heavy petting than with triple-x sex. Indeed, her horror at Arnold Friend's direct solicitation ("I'll come inside you where it's all secret and you'll give in to me and you'll love me—") would appear to be owing to her basic lack of full sexual experience. In the repeated references to rock music in the shopping center she frequents and on the radio, both in Arnold's car and her own house, we find a powerful source of erotic suggestion and of Connie's intensified teen-age hungers, true; but nowhere are we given to feel that she is a fully experienced woman. Rather, we experience her as a somewhat childish and silly narcissistic adolescent, one who feels put down by her more mature older sister (a secretary, and a perfect foil to Connie in her primness) and by her mother, who accuses her of "trashy daydreams." Actually, the trashy daydream involving Arnold may, in a sense, have a certain sobering effect on her frivolousness. Like Dante's dream-vision of Hell, it might improve the situation.

But such speculation begs the question, which is, *Is* it all a daydream? The first clue that we get that it *is* comes even before the Arnold Friend episode, when Oates tells us: "But all the boys fell back and dissolved into a single face that was not even a face but an idea, a feeling, mixed up with the urgent insistent pounding of the music and the humid night air of July." As we shall see, that music provides a key link between her daydreams and their materialization in Arnold Friend. But first we have another important clue, in Connie's languid dreaminess when she is left alone in the house on that fateful, hot summer afternoon: "Connie sat with her eyes closed in the sun, dreaming and dazed with the warmth about her as if this were a kind of love, the caresses of love. . . . She shook her head as if to get awake." Because it is so hot she goes inside and, sitting on the edge of her bed [N.B.], listens for an hour and a half to rock songs on the radio, "bathed in a glow of slow-pulsed joy that seemed to rise mysteriously out of the music itself and lay languidly about the airless little room, breathed in and breathed out with each gentle rise and fall of her chest." At this point Oates starts a new paragraph to tell us that "After a while she heard a car coming up the drive." This is Arnold driving up, just when the author has described certain physiological sounds and motions that sound suspiciously like those of sleep.

If Arnold is indeed the devil—and he may well be, on the level so perspicaciously analyzed by Joyce Wegs—he is certainly a comical one, with his wig, incompletely made-up face, stuffed boots, and stumbling gait. In the *threat* he represents to Connie, of course, he is indeed a figure of evil, but with all this fakery, what Oates seems to be showing us is the absurd emptiness and falseness of sexual fulfillment. Connie fears she will be destroyed by Arnold, and the critics (like Wegs) have concentrated on the immediate level of *physical* death; what makes the story so rich, it seems to me, is the possibility of seeing her pending destruction as a *moral* phenomenon. Her compulsive sex drive will destroy her, Oates seems to tell us, but not simply physically (which, if that were all there were to it, would make the story merely a luscious gumdrop for gothic horror fans). It is the potential destruction of Connie as a *person,* on a humanistic level, that is the real source of power in this story, and it is through the protagonist's daydream of fearful sexual fulfillment that this horror is conveyed.

The fact that Connie recognizes the sensual music being broadcast on Arnold's car radio as being the same as that emanating from her own in the house provides another strong clue to his real nature—that of a dream-like projection of her erotic fantasies. His music and hers, Oates tells us, blend perfectly, and indeed Arnold's voice is perceived by Connie as being the same as that of the disc jockey on the radio. Thus the protagonist's inner state of consciousness is being given physical form by her imagination. We should recall that Connie's initial response to her first view of Arnold the night before, in the shopping center, was one of intense sexual excitement; now she discovers how dangerous that excitement can be to her survival as a person. Instinctively, she recoils; but the conflict between excitement and desire, on the one hand, and fear, on the other, leaves her will paralyzed, and she cannot even dial the phone for help. Such physical paralysis in the

111

face of oncoming danger is a phenomenon familiar to all dreamers, like being unable to run from the monster because your legs won't respond to your will.

Finally, the rather un-devil-like tribute that Arnold pays Connie as she finally succumbs to his threats against her family and goes out of the house to him—". . . you're better than them [her family] because not a one of them would have done this for you"—is exactly what poor, unappreciated Connie wants to hear. She is making a noble sacrifice, and in her dream she gives herself full credit for it.

The episode with Arnold Friend, then, may be viewed as the vehicle for fulfillment of Connie's deep-rooted desire for ultimate sexual gratification, a fearsome business which, for the uninitiated female, may involve destruction of the person. Unsophisticated as she is, Connie's subconscious is aware of this danger, and her dream conveys this conflict. Thus, Oates's achievement in this story lies in her ability to convey all these subtleties while still creating the illusion of a real-life experience.

☐ *Notes* ■

1. Joyce M. Wegs, "'Don't You Know Who I Am?' The Grotesque in Oates's 'Where Are You Going, Where Have You Been?'" See also Joan D. Winslow, "The Stranger Within: Two Stories by Oates and Hawthorne." Both essays are reprinted in this volume.

2. Winslow considers the possibility of the Arnold Friend episode's being interpreted as a dream but focuses primarily on the other similarities between Oates's story and Hawthorne's "Young Goodman Brown."

3. Winslow also discusses the virginal Connie's fear of total sexual experience.

☐ GRETCHEN SCHULZ and R.J.R. ROCKWOOD ■

In Fairyland, without a Map: Connie's Exploration Inward in Joyce Carol Oates's "Where Are You Going, Where Have You Been?"

Joyce Carol Oates has stated that her prize-winning story "Where Are You Going, Where Have You Been?" came to her "more or less in a piece" after hearing Bob Dylan's song "It's All Over Now, Baby Blue," and then reading about a "killer in some Southwestern state," and thinking about "the old legends and folk songs of Death and the Maiden."[1] The "killer" that Miss Oates had in mind, the one on whom her character Arnold Friend is modeled, was twenty-three-year-old Charles Schmid of Tucson, Arizona. Schmid had been charged with the murders of three teen-age girls, and was the subject of a lengthy article in the March 4, 1966, issue of *Life* magazine. It is not surprising that this account should have generated mythic musings in Miss Oates—musings that culminated in a short story which has depths as mythic as any of the "old legends and folk songs." The *Life* reporter, Don Moser, himself had found in this raw material such an abundance of the reality which is the stuff of myth, that he entitled his article "The Pied Piper of Tucson."

The article states that Schmid—or "Smitty," as he was

From *literature and psychology* 30 (1980): 155–167.

called—had sought deliberately "to create an exalted, heroic image of himself." To the teen-agers in Smitty's crowd, who "had little to do but look each other over," their leader was a "folk hero . . . more dramatic, more theatrical, more *interesting* than anyone else in their lives," and seemed to embody the very lyrics of a then popular song: "Hey, c'mon babe, follow me, / I'm the Pied Piper, follow me, / I'm the Pied Piper, / And I'll show you where it's at." With a face which was "his own creation: the hair dyed raven black, the skin darkened to a deep tan with pancake make-up, the lips whitened, the whole effect heightened by a mole he had painted on one cheek," Smitty would cruise "in a golden car," haunting "all the teenage hangouts," looking for pretty girls, especially ones with long blond hair. Because he was only five-foot-three, Smitty "habitually stuffed three or four inches of old rags and tin cans into the bottoms of his high-topped boots to make himself taller," even though the price he paid for that extra height was an awkward, stumbling walk that made people think he had "wooden feet."[2]

In his transformation into the Arnold Friend of "Where Are You Going, Where Have You Been?," Smitty underwent the kind of apotheosis which he had tried, by means of bizarre theatrics, to achieve in actuality, for Arnold is the exact transpersonal counterpart to the real-life "Pied Piper of Tucson." Thus, although Arnold is a "realistic" figure, drawn from the life of a specific psychopathic killer, that superficial realism is only incidental to the more essential realism of the mythic characteristics—the archetypal qualities—he shares with the man who was his model. Asked to comment on Arnold, Miss Oates reveals that, to her, the character is *truly* mythological. No longer quite human, he functions as a personified subjective factor: "Arnold Friend," she says, "is a fantastic figure: he is Death, he is the 'elf-knight' of the ballads, he is the Imagination, he is a Dream, he is a Lover, a Demon, *and all that.*"[3]

If "Where Are You Going, Where Have You Been?" is a "portrait of a psychopathic killer masquerading as a teenager,"[4] it is clear that this portrait is created in the mind of Connie, the teenage protagonist of the story, and that it exists *there only*. It is thus Connie's inner world that determines how Arnold is, or has to be, at least in her eyes, for her personal

114

problems are so compelling that they effectively rearrange and remodel the world of objective reality. Arnold Friend's own part in the creation of his image—whether he deliberately set about to become the "fantastic" figure he is, or seems to be, as his model, Smitty, did—Miss Oates ignores altogether. She is interested only in Connie, Arnold's young victim, and in how Connie's psychological state shapes her perceptions. We find— as we might expect with a writer who characterizes the mode in which she writes as "psychological realism"[5]—that the "fantastic" or mythological qualities of Arnold Friend (and of all those in the story) are presented as subjective rather than objective facts, aspects of the transpersonal psyche projected outward, products of the unconscious mental processes of a troubled adolescent girl.

Toward Arnold Friend, and what he represents, Connie is ambivalent: she is both fascinated and frightened. She is, after all, at that confusing age when a girl feels, thinks, and acts both like a child, put off by a possible lover, and like a woman, attracted to him. Uncertain how to bridge the chasm between "home" and "anywhere that was not home," she stands—or wavers—at the boundary between childhood and adulthood, hesitant and yet anxious to enter the new world of experience which is opening before her:

> Everything about her had two sides to it, one for home and one for anywhere that was not home: her walk, which could be childlike and bobbing, or languid enough to make anyone think she was hearing music in her head; her mouth, which was pale and smirking most of the time, but bright and pink on these evenings out; her laugh, which was cynical and drawling at home—"Ha, ha, very funny,"—but high-pitched and nervous anywhere else, like the jingling of the charms on her bracelet.[6]

That her laugh is "high-pitched and nervous" when she is "anywhere that was not home" betrays the fact that Connie, like all young people, needs help as she begins to move from the past to the future, as she begins the perilous inward journey towards maturity. This journey is an essential part of adolescents' search for personal identity, and though it is a

115

quest that they must undertake by themselves, traditionally it has been the responsibility of culture to help by providing symbolic maps of the territory through which they will travel, territory that lies on the other side of consciousness.

Such models of behavior and maps of the unknown are generally provided by the products of fantasy—myth, legend, and folklore. Folk fairy tales have been especially useful in this way. In his book, *The Uses of Enchantment: The Meaning and Importance of Fairy Tales* (1976), Bruno Bettelheim argues that children's fairy tales offer "symbolic images" that suggest "happy solutions" to the problems of adolescence.[7] Indeed, Joyce Carol Oates herself has Hugh Petrie, the caricaturist in her novel *The Assassins* (1975) observe that "fairy tales are analogous to life as it is lived in the family."[8] In her fiction both short and long Miss Oates makes frequent use of fairy tale material. Again and again she presents characters and situations which parallel corresponding motifs from the world of folk fantasy. And never is this more true than in the present story—never in all the novels and collections of short stories which she has written at last count. Woven into the complex texture of "Where Are You Going, Where Have You Been?" are motifs from such tales as "The Spirit in the Bottle," "Snow White," "Cinderella," "Sleeping Beauty," "Rapunzel," "Little Red Riding Hood," and "The Three Little Pigs."[9] *The Pied Piper of Hamelin,* which ends tragically and so according to Bettelheim does not qualify as a proper fairy tale, serves as the "frame device" that contains all the other tales.[10]

There is a terrible irony here, for although the story is full of fairy tales, Connie, its protagonist, is not. Connie represents an entire generation of young people who have grown up—or tried to—without the help of those bedtime stories which not only entertain the child, but also enable him vicariously to experience and work through problems which he will encounter in adolescence. The only "stories" Connie knows are those of the sexually provocative but superficial lyrics of the popular songs she loves or of the equally insubstantial movies she attends. Such songs and movies provide either no models of behavior for her to imitate, or dangerously inappropriate ones. Connie has thus been led to believe that life and, in particular, love will be "sweet, gentle, the way it was in the movies and promised in songs." She has no idea that life actually can be just as grim as in folk fairy tales. The society that is depicted in "Where Are You Going, Where Have You Been?" has failed to make available to children like Connie maps of the unconscious such as fairy tales provide, because it has failed to recognize that in the unconscious past and future coalesce, and that, psychologically, where the child is going is where he has already been. Since Connie has been left—in the words of yet another of the popular songs—to "wander through that wonderland alone"—, it is small wonder, considering her lack of spiritual preparation, that Connie's journey there soon becomes a terrifying schizophrenic separation from reality, with prognosis for recovery extremely poor.

The fact that the Oates story, like the magazine article which inspired it, is framed around the motif of the Pied Piper is significant, for this device serves to fix blame for the catastrophe which the story describes. The motif suggests that the adults of Connie's world have made the same mistake as the Burghers of Hamelin seven centuries before: having failed to live up to their moral obligations by refusing to "pay the piper," they themselves—albeit unknowingly—have unleashed the very force which will prove destructive to their children. What kind of force this is, and its particular implications for Connie, we can understand more clearly by interpreting the symbolism underlying the fate of the legendary children of Hamelin: led outside the comfortable sanity of their walled city, the children disappear into that emblem of the devouring unconscious, the Koppenberg ('head mountain'), victims, we would say, of an acute, collective psychosis. Assuming that the eternal patterns recur, each time as though for the first and last time, then this will be Connie's fate too, and her own psychosis will likewise have no remission. Certainly Arnold Friend is such that Connie cannot keep from following him, perhaps because in following him she is following the popular music she loves, music with which he is not only closely identified, but of which he is the personification. Thus, when Connie, "hearing music in her head," wanders into the bottle-shaped drive-in restaurant, charmed by "the music that made everything so good: the music . . . always in the background, like music at a church service," it is there that she first sees him. He later arrives at her house with a transistor radio which is playing "the same program that was playing inside the house," a program which leaves Connie feeling "bathed in a glow of slow-pulsed joy that seemed to rise mysteriously out of the music itself." Arnold even talks in a "simple lilting voice, exactly as if he were reciting the words to a song." There are many more passages of this kind, but let these suffice to show that Arnold is, indeed, depicted as a Pied Piper, incarnated by society's refusal to live up to its cultural obligation to provide what is needed to help the adolescent make it safely through to adulthood.

The help provided by fairy tales proper is such that a child can learn to compensate even when adult society makes errors of the gravest sort, capping with a happy ending a situation which might otherwise prove tragic for the child. Accordingly, the force which lures all save one of the unwitting children of Hamelin to their psychological death in the Koppenberg[11] is identical to that which the child is taught to tame in the fairy tale *Spirit in the Bottle*. For Connie, the "bottle" is the drive-in restaurant where the teen-agers hang out, a restaurant "shaped like a big bottle, though squatter than a real bottle . . . [and] on its cap a revolving figure of a grinning boy holding a hamburger aloft." The boy on the bottlecap reminds us of "the boy named Eddie" inside the restaurant who, appropriately, sits *eddying* on his stool, "turning himself jerkily around in semi-circles and then stopping and turning back again," motion which suggests that bottled up sexual pressures are building, ever more insistent in their demand for release. Eddie takes Connie off for some petting, some rubbing that arouses her sexuality, too, until in her mind his face dissolves "into a single face that was not even a face but an idea, a feeling, mixed up with the urgent insistent pounding of the music and the humid night air of July." On this same visit to the restaurant Connie arouses Arnold Friend, who wags his finger at her, laughs, and says, "'Gonna get you, baby'," and who at this moment reveals that he is not only the Pied Piper, but also that hostile spirit in the bottle which is described in the fairy tale.

When the woodcutter's son discovers *his* mysterious bottle and releases a spirit which likewise threatens to destroy

118

him, he manages to entrap the spirit once again, agreeing to release it only when it agrees to share its special powers with him, powers which enable the boy to become the "greatest physician in the land." As in the fairy tale, Connie has uncorked the bottle, but because she is unacquainted with this part of the psyche, she is not equipped to recognize the grinning boy atop the bottle-cap or the laughing Arnold Friend as a potentially destructive force which must be controlled if it is to make a positive contribution to her personality. What complicates the attempt to control this force is that it disguises itself as mere sexuality, as is evident from the fairy tale in the fact that the bottle is clearly phallic and the boy's handling of it masturbatory: if we consider that what leads to the boy's taking flight and finding the bottle is his father's belittling him for incompetence at chopping wood, we can say that, psychologically, the boy is seeking compensation in an eroticised flood of negative content from the unconscious. Bettelheim points out that a fairy tale like "Spirit in the Bottle" deals with two problems that confront the child as he struggles to establish a sense of identity: parental belittlement, and integration of a divided personality.[12] In Connie's case, her mother's belittling remarks that "Connie couldn't do a thing, her mind was all filled with trashy daydreams," certainly have contributed to Connie's two-sidedness, with her one personality "for home" and another for "anywhere that was not home," a division also apparent in the relationship between Connie and the "girl friend" who accompanies her to the bottle-shaped restaurant—the two are so poorly differentiated as to suggest a mere *doubling* of Connie, rather than two separate individuals. While such personality division may at first glance seem pathological, it is not, according to Bettelheim, necessarily abnormal, since "the manner in which the child can bring some order into his world view is by dividing everything into opposites," and that "in the later oedipal and post oedipal ages, this splitting extends to the child himself."[13] In "Spirit in the Bottle," the degraded hero, reacting to the anguish of being regarded by his parent as stupid and incompetent, withdraws into himself, undergoes a split into positive and negative aspects, de-energizes the negative (as represented by the spirit that comes out of the bottle), and then successfully reintegrates his personality, achieving a durable and socially productive synthesis. Had Connie been familiar with this fairy tale, she would have known that however deplorable her situation might seem at a given moment, the means toward an eventual happy solution is in learning to interact with the unconscious in such a way as to emulate the woodcutter's son, who, *by asserting rational control over the terms of the spirit's release into consciousness,* is able to demonstrate to himself and the world that he is not only wiser and better than his parent, but positively the "greatest physician in the land."

Knowledge of this tale alone, however, would not suffice, for it is merely a beginning: to be assured of safe passage through what Bettelheim terms "that thorniest of thickets, the oedipal period,"[14] a child like Connie would need to have absorbed the wisdom of the other fairy tales to which Miss Oates alludes, tales such as "Snow White," "Cinderella," "Rapunzel," and "Little Red Riding Hood." By their applicability to Connie's situation, these tales reveal that at its deepest level Connie's most compelling psychological problem is *unresolved oedipal conflict, aggravated by sibling rivalry.*

Suggestive of "Snow White" is Connie's "habit of craning her neck to glance into mirrors, or checking other people's faces to make sure her own was all right" (as though other people's faces were mirrors, too); and we are told also that her mother, "who noticed everything and knew everything"— as though with the wicked queen's magic power—"hadn't much reason any longer to look at her own face," and so was jealous of her daughter's beauty and "always after Connie." Arnold Friend's sunglasses also mirror everything, which means that, in this instance, he personifies the Magic Mirror and, of course, he finds Connie the fairest one of all. In his words, "Seen you that night and thought, that's the one, yes sir, I never needed to look anymore." Though he thus serves as Prince, there is a hint of the dwarf motif in Arnold's short stature and obvious phallicism; and most particularly is this true of his friend, Ellie Oscar, a case of arrested development, whose face is that of a "forty-year-old baby." Connie's "Someday My Prince Will Come" daydreams, plus the many references to how dazed and sleepy she always is, especially the day Arnold comes for her, when she "lay languidly about the airless little room" and "breathed in and breathed out with each gentle rise and fall of her chest"—these, too, suggest "Snow White" and, for that matter, "Sleeping Beauty," whose heroine in the Brothers Grimm is, like Connie, fifteen.

The oedipal implications of "Snow White" are evident in the fact that, as Bettelheim points out, the queen's Magic Mirror speaks not with the mother's but the daughter's voice, revealing the jealous child's own sense of inferiority and frustration projected onto her mother. The father's romantic feelings for the daughter are never at issue in such a fairy tale, and he is generally depicted as weak, ineffectual, and oblivious to the struggle that issues between mother and daughter[15]—exactly as in Miss Oates's story:

> Their father was away at work most of the time and when he came home he wanted supper and he read the newspaper at supper and after supper he went to bed. He didn't bother talking much to them, but around his bent head Connie's mother kept picking at her until Connie wished her mother was dead and she herself was dead and it was all over.

It would be difficult to find a more striking emblem of mother-daughter oedipal conflict than in this passage, where the second death wish serves as punishment for the first.

Bettelheim observes that whenever the child's feeling of "degradation" is the result of "oedipal entanglement of father and daughter," the "Cinderella" theme emerges.[16] Unlike "Snow White," however, "Cinderella" centers on the "agonies and hopes which form the essential content of sibling rivalry . . . [since] 'having lived among the ashes' was a symbol of being debased in comparison to one's siblings."[17] In this case, the relationship between Connie and her sister June is a classical statement of the pattern:

> Her sister June was twenty-four and still lived at home. She was a secretary in the high school Connie attended, and if that wasn't bad enough—with her in the same building—she was so plain and chunky and steady that Connie had to hear her praised all the time by her mother and her mother's sisters. June did this, June did that . . .

Although grown up, June has not only not left home, but, in a sense, she is still in high school: this suggests that June is an even greater victim of oedipal entanglement than Connie—or, to put it another way, that June is Connie projected nine years into the future. What we have is thus a feminine version of the tale "Two Brothers" in which the personality is split between "striving for independence and self-assertion" (Connie) and "the opposite tendency to remain safely home, tied to the parents" (June).[18] Implied also is the dichotomy underlying "Sinbad the Seaman and Sinbad the Porter," in which the former character represents the "pleasure-oriented id" (Connie) and the latter the "reality-oriented ego" (June).[19] In this instance the ego is oriented toward the reality of permanent oedipal fixation, and therefore constitutes a negative personality, conforming to the Jungian concept of the *shadow*.[20] Perhaps the saddest commentary on the situation in Miss Oates's story is the fact that the personality receiving positive reinforcement is Connie's shadow: "If June's name was mentioned her mother's tone was approving, and if Connie's name was mentioned it was disapproving."

The theme of debasement with respect to one's siblings is, of course, not the only link between this story and "Cinderella." Connie, with her other personality for "anywhere that was not home," suggests "Cinderella" too, especially in the magical transformation from child to woman which she undergoes on her nights out. The description of the drive-in restaurant, with its music, and the boys with whom the girls pair up, and their feeling that the event is a wonderful experience, which must end too soon—all of this brings to mind Cinderella's ball, particularly since it is here that Connie meets Arnold Friend, her "Prince Charming." And it is this meeting which sends him seeking her out and finding her, barefoot, in the kitchen. Certainly the "convertible jalopy painted gold" suggests "Cinderella," though in the fairy tale it is Cinderella herself who has the "convertible" vehicle. This gold-painted car reminds us of a royal chariot, too, especially with the horn sounding as though to announce the arrival of royalty when the car comes up Connie's drive. Still more obvious in its reference to the fairy tale is the drawing on the car of "a round, grinning face that reminded Connie of a pumpkin, except it wore sunglasses" and was signed "ARNOLD FRIEND." It is also pertinent that Arnold proclaims that he has come to take her away, and that, as he talks, Connie notices "He had the voice of the man on the radio now," a man who has been mentioned several times, whose name suggests royalty epitomized, a man called "Bobby King."

If Connie is Cinderella, she is also, by virtue of her "long dark blond hair that drew anyone's eye to it," Rapunzel. On the day of Arnold's arrival, Connie "washed her hair so that it could dry all day long in the sun."

At the first sound of the car, "her fingers snatched at her hair, checking it, and she whispered, 'Christ, Christ,' wondering how she looked." While she talks with Arnold, she makes the most of her hair: "Connie smirked and let her hair fall loose over one shoulder." Later, frightened by the desire she has aroused in him, she argues that her father is coming back to the house for her, that she has had to wash her hair in preparation for his return, but Arnold says, "No, your daddy is not coming and yes, you had to wash your hair and you washed it for me. It's nice and shining and all for me. I thank you sweetheart." Again, at the very end of the story, Connie watches "this body and this head of long hair moving out into the sunlight where Arnold Friend waited." It is obvious that Connie's *crowning glory* is, indeed, her hair, that she uses it to draw boys to her, among them Arnold Friend, and that Arnold, like the Prince in the fairy tale, takes her away from a place where she feels "locked inside." The fact that in the fairy tale the Prince is temporarily blinded by thorns when he falls from the tower where Rapunzel is locked is perhaps echoed in Arnold's peculiar eyes, "like holes . . . like chips of broken glass," which he covers with those dark glasses.

Why Arnold Friend is conjured up when it is, as she claims, her father that Connie is waiting for, becomes clear if we consider that Arnold, the Prince of "Snow White," "Sleeping Beauty," "Cinderella," and "Rapunzel" is also the Big Bad Wolf of "Little Red Riding Hood," a tale which, according to Bettelheim, "deals with the daughter's unconscious wish to be seduced by her father (the wolf)."[21] If Arnold represents an erotic transformation of Connie's father, then this suggests that Connie's oedipal death-wish for her mother has undergone psychological realization. This in turn sheds light on that curious conversation between Arnold and Connie concerning "that old woman down the road" whom Connie insists is dead ("'She's dead—she's—she isn't here any more—'"), but about whom Arnold says, "'But don't you like her, I mean, you got something against her? Some grudge or something?'" Connie's overreaction, so revealing in its guilt and terror, tells us that she has displaced onto the "old woman" the homicidal impulses unconsciously intended for her mother, an indiscretion for which she is already punishing herself through Arnold Friend. Bettelheim observes that when Little Red Riding Hood is swallowed up by the wolf, she is being "punished for arranging for the wolf to do away with a mother figure."[22]

Since one of Arnold's more lupine characteristics is his *hairiness,* it is odd, though appropriate psychologically, considering that Arnold is experienced as a transformation of her "nice old bald-headed daddy," that Connie cannot keep from seeing "as a wig" Arnold's shaggy, shabby black hair. But Arnold's hairiness is not the only sign that Connie's daddy-substitute is wolvish. He also has trouble standing and moving about, which suggests a four-footed animal masquerading as a man. When he first gets out of his car, he moves "carefully, planting his feet firmly on the ground." Later, he stands "in a strange way, leaning back against the car as if he were balancing himself." Later still, "He wobble[s] in his high boots and grab[s] hold of one of the porch posts." No wonder Connie has the uneasy feeling that "his feet do not go all the way down" into those boots as they should. Then, of course, there are Arnold's teeth, so "big and white," and his way of "sniffing" at Connie as though "she were a treat he was going to gobble up." What could be more reminiscent of the Wolf in "Little Red Riding Hood?" And we should add that Arnold's talk of tearing Connie's house down reminds us of the Wolf in "The Three Little Pigs," also. When Connie tries to lock the screen door, Arnold says:

> But why lock it . . . It's just a screen door. It's just nothing . . .
> I mean, anybody can break through a screen door and glass
> and wood and iron or anything else if he needs to, anybody at

all, and specially Arnold Friend. If the place got lit up with a fire, honey, you'd come runnin' out into my arms.

Later, in a statement that accurately epitomizes Connie's entire situation, he says: "'This place you are now—inside your daddy's house—is nothing but a cardboard box I can knock down any time. You know that and always did know it'."

If the structure of Connie's life—and of her psyche— were not, indeed, as flimsy as cardboard, she might be able to deal with Arnold Friend even as Beauty deals with the Beast who is *her* daddy-substitute; she might learn to love him for himself and so transform him into a Prince again. But Connie lacks the familial and psychic strength which allows Beauty and her love to mature.[23] She is still just as "little" as Little Red Riding Hood. And, as we shall see, her confrontation with "the Beast"—with the wolvish Arnold Friend—makes her more childlike, not less; she regresses to what Bettelheim describes as a "more primitive, earlier form of existence,"[24] as Red Riding Hood does under similar circumstances. Of course, "in typical fairystory fashion" Red Riding Hood's regression is "impressively exaggerated." She goes all the way back to "the pre-birth existence in the womb" when she is swallowed by the Wolf (an act which has sexual significance, too). And she must then be cut from that "womb" by the Woodcutter, to emerge as a "born again" Red Riding Hood, a child who has learned that she is a child and still too young to deal with the Wolf.[25] Miss Oates is not free to exaggerate so fantastically, but she can and does suggest that Connie's psychological experience parallels Red Riding Hood's—in all respects save one. In Connie's case, Arnold Friend is the Woodcutter as well as the Wolf.

Connie begins to regress to a more childlike state as soon as she realizes that Arnold is more Wolf than Prince, more interested in animal sex than happy-ever-after romance. When he suddenly announces, "'I'm your lover. You don't know what that is yet but you will'," she is frightened, and when he proceeds to explain "what that is" in some detail, she is more frightened still. Her flirtatious words and gestures give way to the frantic words and gestures of a child—and a very young child at that: "'Shut up! You're crazy!' Connie said. . . . She put her hands up against her ears as if she'd heard something terrible, something not meant for her. 'People don't talk like that, you're crazy,' she muttered." Furthermore, while she is saying this, she "back[s] away from the door," and so backs away from that symbolic threshold between "home" and "not home," childhood and womanhood, where she has been hovering ever since Arnold arrived. She has not locked the door, though, and when she remembers that fact and tries to do so, with fingers clumsy as a child's, she fails. A "wave of dizziness and fear" has left her sweating, "panting," "shaking"—utterly unable to save herself from the Wolf. Of course, we must not forget that this Wolf actually embodies Connie's own sexual impulses, a fact which implies that her childlike inability to save herself from him is complicated by a womanly desire to give herself to him. And, indeed, the very portions of the text which suggest that Connie is feeling like a terrified child simultaneously suggest that she is feeling like a woman thoroughly aroused by Arnold Friend and the sex he offers. The "wave of dizziness," the sweating, "panting," and "shaking" all characterize a woman well on the way to orgasm.

Connie's progression towards orgasm and her regression towards the womb both reach their climax in that decidedly schizophrenic moment when she tries to call her mother on the telephone. Miss Oates describes it thus:

> . . . she ran into the back room and picked up the telephone. Something roared in her ear, a tiny roaring, and she was so sick with fear that she could do nothing but listen to it—the telephone was clammy and very heavy and her fingers groped down to the dial but were too weak to touch it. She began to scream into the phone, into the roaring. She cried out, she cried for her mother, she felt her breath start jerking back and forth in her lungs as if it were something Arnold Friend was stabbing her with again and again with no tenderness. A noisy sorrowful wailing rose all about her and she was locked inside it the way she was locked inside this house.
>
> After a while she could hear again. She was sitting on the floor with her wet back against the wall.

If the spasms which set Connie's "breath . . . jerking back and forth" as if Arnold were "stabbing her . . . again and again" suggest that she is experiencing something like the moment of climax in the sexual act, they also indicate that she is succumbing to sexual appetite exactly as Red Riding Hood does when she climbs into bed with the Wolf. Of course, Red Riding Hood is seeking the safety of a mother-figure's arms, the safety of a womb, not sex. This is true of Connie, too. The little girl in her is acting littler all the time, and now, more like a baby than a child, she is crying for her mother, trying to reach her mother through the umbilical-like cord on a phone she has forgotten how to use. She cannot reach her mother, but she does manage to reach the momentary safety of a womb of sorts. The lines which suggest that she is experiencing something like orgasm also suggest that she is experiencing something like birth—but in reverse. The description of the "breath . . . jerking back and forth in her lungs" in spasms that set her "wailing" reminds us of the moment of birth; and it is followed by a description that makes Connie sound like an unborn baby (rather than a newborn one), for she collapses into an unconscious and embryonic heap on the floor of the house where she feels "locked inside," even as a baby is "locked inside" a womb.

Connie does not stay in that "womb," however. The child in Connie may want to stay there, but the woman in Connie wants to be born. And the same spasms that suggest a birth-in-reverse suggest a birth-in-progress, too, a birth in which the two Connies who have thus far existed together in the one Connie, with the woman "locked inside" the womb of the child, are finally torn apart. As the story moves toward its conclusion, we note that the child who has thus become mother of the woman feels "hollow." She feels as if her "heart" and "body" are not "really hers" any more. They belong to that womanly part of her which now seems to be someone else entirely—someone who pushes her way out of the womb-like house where she has spent her formative years even as she has pushed her way out of the womb of the child:

> She put out her hand against the screen. She watched herself push the door slowly open as if she were back safe somewhere

inside the house . . . watching this body and this head of long
hair moving out into the sunlight where Arnold Friend waited.

Arnold Friend has not had to pull Connie out of the womb with
the physical force which the Woodcutter uses in the fairy tale.
We should remember that he has threatened to use such
physical force if necessary, but his psychological force (as an
embodiment of Connie's own impulses) proves to be more
than sufficient to ensure that the birth takes place, whether
the embryonic woman is really ready to be born or not.

Of course she is not ready to be born—despite the fact
that it is only as a newborn that brown-eyed Connie can be
Arnold's "sweet little blue-eyed girl." Connie has not developed enough to survive in the world outside the womb—in the
world outside the conscious personality—and it is not surprising that she gazes upon this world in utter bewilderment:
"—so much land that Connie had never seen before and did
not recognize except to know that she was going to it."[26] Had
she been nurtured on fairy tales instead of popular songs and
movies she would not feel at such a loss; she would have
"been" to this world before, through the vicarious experience
offered by fairy tales, and she would have some sense of how
to survive there now. Connie lacks the benefit of such experience, however, and even Arnold Friend appears to realize how
that lack has hampered her development. He certainly speaks
to the supposed woman as though she were still a child:
"'Now, turn this way. That's right. Come over here to me. . . .
and let's see a smile, try it, you're a brave, sweet little girl'."
How fatherly he sounds. And how like the Woodcutter. But we
know that he is still the Wolf, and that he still intends to
"gobble up" this "little girl" as soon as he gets the chance.
Connie is not going to live happily ever after. Indeed, it would
seem that she is not going to live at all. She simply does not
know how. She is stranded in Fairyland, without a map.[27]

☐ Notes ■

1. Interview with Joyce Carol Oates about "Where Are You
Going, Where Have You Been?" in *Mirrors: An Introduction to Lit-*

erature, ed. John R. Knott, Jr., and Christopher R. Keaske, 2nd ed. (San Francisco: Canfield Press, 1975), pp. 18–19.

2. Don Moser, "The Pied Piper of Tucson," *Life* (March 4, 1966). Reprinted in this volume.

3. Interview in *Mirrors*, p. 19. For a perceptive analysis of Arnold Friend as a demonic figure, a subject which will not be developed here, see Joyce M. Wegs, "Don't You Know Who I Am?: The Grotesque in Oates's 'Where Are You Going, Where Have You Been?'." Reprinted in this volume.

4. Wegs, "Don't You Know Who I Am?"

5. Joyce Carol Oates, "Preface," *Where Are You Going, Where Have You Been?: Stories of Young America* (Greenwich, Conn.: Fawcett Publications, 1974), p. 10.

6. The story was originally published in *Epoch*, Fall 1966. It has since been included in *Prize Stories: The O. Henry Awards 1968;* in *The Best American Short Stories of 1967;* and in a collection of Oates' stories, *The Wheel of Love* (New York: Vanguard Press, 1970; New York: Fawcett Publications, 1972). The story is also being anthologized with increasing frequency in collections intended for use in the classroom, such as Donald McQuade and Robert Atwan, *Popular Writing in America: The Interaction of Style and Audience* (New York: Oxford University Press, 1974).

7. Bruno Bettelheim, *The Uses of Enchantment: The Meaning and Importance of Fairy Tales* (New York: Alfred A. Knopf, 1976), p. 39.

8. Joyce Carol Oates, *The Assassins* (New York: Vanguard Press, 1975), p. 378.

9. At the MLA convention in New York, on December 26, 1976, I got a chance to ask Joyce Carol Oates if the many allusions to various fairy tales in *Where Are You Going, Where Have You Been?* were intentional. She replied that they were. (Gretchen Schulz)

10. Bettelheim, n. 34, p. 316.

11. According to the legend, one of the children of Hamelin does survive, though against his will. He is a *lame* boy who falls so far behind the other children that before he can reach the opening into the Koppenberg, it closes, swallowing all but himself. Psychologically, the boy's "lameness" can be interpreted as an unconscious protective mechanism which is capable of thwarting the boy's conscious will, thus saving him from destruction. This is protection exactly of the sort that properly internalized fairy tales provide, and

its chief advantage is that it is not subject to the ego's often erring judgment, since it operates beyond the effective jurisdiction of consciousness.

12. Bettelheim, pp. 66 ff.; n. 6, pp. 311–312; and *passim.*

13. Bettelheim, p. 74.

14. Bettelheim, p. 73.

15. Bettelheim, pp. 207, 114.

16. Bettelheim, p. 245.

17. Bettelheim, p. 236.

18. Bettelheim, p. 91.

19. Bettelheim, p. 85.

20. C. G. Jung, *The Archetypes and the Collective Unconscious,* 2nd ed., and *Aion,* 2nd ed., Collected Works of C. G. Jung, Vol. IX, pts. I & II (Princeton, N.J.: Princeton University Press, 1968), *passim.*

21. Bettelheim, p. 175.

22. Bettelheim, p. 172.

23. Bettelheim, pp. 303–309, *passim.*

24. Bettelheim, p. 180.

25. Bettelheim, p. 180.

26. There is a fascinating and, it seems, rather significant echo between this line and the passage in Hemingway's *The Snows of Kilimanjaro,* where at the moment of his death from gangrene, Harry imagines that the overdue plane that was to take him to the hospital in Arusha arrives, and shortly after taking off with Harry aboard, turns to the left (away from Arusha), and heads instead for the summit of Mt. Kilimanjaro: "Then they began to climb and they were going to the East it seemed, and then it darkened and they were in a storm, the rain so thick it seemed like flying through a waterfall, and then they were out and Compie (the pilot) turned his head and grinned and pointed and there, ahead, all he could see, as wide as all the world, great, high, and unbelievably white in the sun, was the square top of Kilimanjaro. *And then he knew that there was where he was going* [italics mine]." Ernest Hemingway, "The Snows of Kilimanjaro," *The Fifth Column and the First Forty-nine Stories* (New York: Charles Scribner's Sons, 1938), p. 174.

27. Concerning the plight of the Connies of the world, Bettelheim states thus: ". . . unfed by our common fantasy heritage, the folk fairy tale, the child cannot invent stories on his own which help

him cope with life's problems. All the stories he can invent are just expressions of his own wishes and anxieties. Relying on his own resources, all the child can imagine are elaborations of where he presently is, since he cannot know where he needs to go, or how to go about getting there." (pp. 121–122)

"Where Are You Going, Where Have You Been?": Seduction, Space, and a Fictional Mode

Joyce Carol Oates's "Where Are You Going, Where Have You Been?" is a story about beginnings and passage points; and it is a story about endings: the end of childhood, the end of innocence. The account of fifteen-year-old Connie's encounter with a mysterious stranger named Arnold Friend, a man who leads his victim not to a promising new world, but, rather, to a violent sexual assault, is a tale of initiation depicted in grotesque relief.

But "Where Are You Going" is also a story where spatial limitations are of crucial concern, and to this degree it provides a commentary on stories and story-telling. As Oates transforms elements of fairy tale and dream into a chilling description of temptation, seduction, and probable rape, we are forced to consider the distinctions between fairy tale and seduction narrative, to note particularly that in "Where Are You Going" seduction involves the invasion of personal, interior space: ". . . his words, replete with guild, / Into her heart too easy entrance won," Milton says of Satan's meeting with Eve in Book IX *Paradise Lost*. Women are vulnerable to seduction, and of course rape, Susan Brownmiller has reminded us, for

---

From *Studies in Short Fiction* 18 (1981): 65–70.

what at first may be seen as purely physiological reasons;[1] and there is little doubt of physical violence when Arnold Friend croons to Connie, "I'll come inside you where it's all secret"; but the seduction motif functions so successfully in "Where Are You Going" because the delineation of interior space figured in the female body analogizes invasion at several levels; the domestic space, the state of childhood associated with the home, and, of course, the individual consciousness.

Following the example of the eighteenth-century seduction tale, Oates takes us *within* her story, pointing up one direction which fiction has taken for some two hundred years. In the transformation of romance into sentimental narrative, the seduction of the inexperienced young woman depends in part upon the demarcation of interior space and the importance of maintaining it intact. More specifically, too, private space is congruent with the domestic. In painting, the conversation piece shows us the family unit within its drawing room, closed off from an outside world; sentimental drama draws us within to witness the distresses of private persons in familial surroundings; and seduction narratives which stress the strength of the virtuous daughter in warding off the dangerous rake similarly suggest the importance of protecting both the physical body and the nuclear family.[2] In this sense, we may speak of the domestication or privatization of sin in eighteenth-century literature: in a world which historian Lawrence Stone has described as ever more conscious of private space we are not surprised to find fictions turning toward the exploration of private zones and evil represented as that which threatens the privacy of self and the family unit.[3] Readers may now penetrate the locus of private, familial activity, the consciousness of the fictionalized character, and the pages of the text they are reading. The theme of the young lady's "entering the world" (to quote Fanny Burney's *Evelina* and a score of so-called "female" fictions)—or perhaps, like Clarissa Harlowe, her seduction into the "world"—provides a context within which we may consider how Oates's Connie is "invaded" and where she may indeed be going.

At the outset we may identify "Where Are You Going" as an American "coming of age" tale, the main character Connie joining that cast of characters which includes Huckleberry

Finn, Isabel Archer, and Jay Gatsby. But while the poles of Oates's story are innocence and experience, the focus of attention is the process of seduction, or the threshold between the two states. The lines are clear, the threshold visually realized. Connie belongs to a tradition of domesticated Eves; for them, Satan's entrance into the garden is replaced by the invasion of a rake like Lovelace (in Richardson's *Clarissa*) into one's private chamber—or ultimately, in the twentieth century, by the approach of the cowboy-booted Arnold Friend to the kitchen door of an asbestos-covered ranch house. The physical world shrinks in this fiction; unlike Eden, the perimeter of a private room, or body, lends itself to specific accounting. Within a described locus, space itself is at issue, the fiction setting up a tension whereby the private is open to both attack and transformation.

Spatial limits are increasingly important in "Where Are You Going." If the threshold of the kitchen door ultimately receives the burden of tension in the tale, Oates carefully prepares us for the climactic scene by setting up, at the outset, contrasting *loci*. The very title of the story calls attention to duality: a future (where you are going) and a past (where you have been). The tale catches its main character at a passage point where, it is implied, the future may depend precipitously on the past. More specifically, the two major locations of the tale are the home and family unit it signifies, and the outside world represented first in the drive-in hamburger joint, later in Arnold Friend himself. Connie herself lives in two worlds, even dressing appropriately for each: she "wore a pull over jersey blouse that looked one way when she was at home and another way when she was away from home. Everything about her had two sides to it, one for home and one for anywhere that was not home." Home is the daylight world, a known, established order where so-called parental wisdom would seem to negate the dreams and desires of youth. Connie is, then, constantly at odds with her family, ever looking forward to her excursions to the drive-in, the night-time world, the "bright-lit, fly-infested restaurant" which she and her friend approach, "their faces pleased and expectant as if they were entering a sacred building that loomed up out of the night to give them what haven and blessing they yearned for."

135

A mood of expectation pervades Connie's night-time world. Like the light on Daisy Buchanan's pier that promised romance to Jay Gatsby, the bright-lit hamburger joint also holds out new worlds within its "sacred" precincts: cars, music, boys, experience.

Even when the initial meeting with a boy named Eddie—the experience "down the alley a mile or so away"—is over, when the clock has struck eleven and the Cinderella land fades back into the night, a "bit empty parking lot [with] signs that were faded and ghostly," even then, the mood of expectation is only temporarily broken. There will be other nights in this midsummer dream-time. Eddie and his like, all the boys, Oates tells us, "fell back and dissolved into a single face that was not even a face but an idea, a feeling, mixed up with the urgent insistent pounding of the music and humid air of July." No wonder that Connie resists being "dragged back to the daylight" by her mother's too-insistent voice. The mother who had once been pretty ("but now her looks were gone and that was why she was always after Connie") sees in Connie a dim outline of her own former self; but the dream perception seems long faded, and Connie's sister June, the only other female member, is a plain, stalwart sort who has clearly never had much to do with dreams.

But mother and sister are not the villains here, of course, Connie no Cinderella for whom a night-time dream becomes daylight reality. Rather, dream becomes nightmare when Connie first meets at the drive-in Arnold Friend, no Prince Charming, but a man with metallic, cold eyes, driving a bright gold jalopy. And Arnold Friend only pretends to be young. Later, with the discovery of Arnold's true age, Connie will feel her heart pound faster; the bizarre realization that Friend's companion has the face of a "forty year old baby" will cause the teenager to experience a "wave of dizziness." And we are shocked too: there is no fairy tale world here, no romance after all. Friend's first muttered threat, "Gonna get you, baby," is to be played out not in a dream, but in the daylight hours and within a domestic space.

Even before Arnold Friend's entrance into the driveway of Connie's home, reality and dream are beginning to clash

136

dangerously. Connie sits in the sun "dreaming and dazed with the warmth about her as if this were a kind of love, the caresses of love;" but when she opens her eyes she sees only a "back yard that ran off into weeds" and a house that looked small. Arnold's appearance in Connie's driveway on the Sunday morning when her family have gone off to a barbecue only underlines the confused merging of two worlds Connie has always kept apart. She approaches the kitchen door slowly, hangs out the screen door, "her bare toes curling down off the step." Connie is not yet ready to make the step outside.

With Arnold's arrival the significance of separate locations in "Where Are You Going" acquires new intensity, and the delineation of space becomes a matter of crucial concern. Connie's refusal to move down off the step bespeaks her clinging to a notion that walls and exact locations offer the protection of the familial order. Now, with Friend's initial invitation to join him and his friend in the car, and with his assertion that he has placed his "sign" upon her, Connie moves further back into the kitchen: she "let the screen door close and stood perfectly still inside it." From the familiar kitchen space, she attempts to make sense of her experience. But the mirror sunglasses make it impossible for the girl to see what Friend is looking at; the enigmatic smile tells nothing; and even as she attempts to amass assorted physical data on her visitor, she finds that "all these things did not come together."

Then the familiar and the private began to give way to the unexpected visitor. Having realized the true age of the two intruders and being told that they will not leave until she agrees to go along with them, Connie has the sense that Friend "had driven up the driveway all right but had come from nowhere before and belonged nowhere . . . everything that was so familiar to her was only half real." The drawing of the magical sign, a sign of ownership over her, suggests control over her own private consciousness. Connie wonders how Friend knows her name; but later, much more troubling, is his knowledge that her father is not coming back soon, that the family is at the picnic. Connie finds herself sharing a perhaps imaginary, perhaps real, view of the barbecue. Friend refers to a "fat woman" at the barbecue:

"What fat woman?" Connie cried.

"How do I know what fat woman. I don't know every god-damn fat woman in the world!" Arnold Friend laughed.

"Oh, that's Mrs. Hornsby. . . . Who invited her?" Connie said. She felt a little lightheaded. Her breath was coming quickly.

And penetration of consciousness is only the preamble to penetration in a sexual sense: "And I'll come inside you where it's all secret and you'll give in to me and you'll love me—" says Friend. The disorder implied in Friend's knowing too much, more than can be rationally explained, is now to be played out in trespassing upon the body itself. A limit has been passed. Connie does not want to hear these words; she "backed away from the door. She put her hand up against her ears as if she'd heard something terrible."

Connie retreats further within the kitchen, but the space of the room also loses familiarity as interior worlds break down. Just as earlier in the morning the adolescent has begun to see her own home as small, now the kitchen looked "like a place she had never seen before, some room she had run inside but that wasn't good enough, wasn't going to help her." Doors too become meaningless. "But why lock [the door]?" Friend taunts; "it's just a screen door. It's just nothing." Friend is still articulating spatial limits—"[I] promise not to come in unless you touch the phone"—but such limits no longer have meaning. The statement, "I want you," the words of the teen-ager's love song, now connote a world where the limits around self are not viable. The breaking of a limitation and the opening of a door (here is the language which Richardson used in reference to the rape of Clarissa Harlowe, and here are Richardson's issues too) destroy both individual innocence and the order of the innocent's world. "It's all over for you here," Friend tells Connie. Crying out for the mother that will not come, Connie feels not the protective parental embrace, but rather a feeling in her lungs as if Friend "was stabbing her . . . with no tenderness." And then the horrible statement muttered in a stage voice, the statement which spells the end of a world: "The place where you came from ain't there any more, and where you had in mind to go is cancelled out. This place you are now—inside your daddy's house—is nothing but a cardboard box I can knock down any time."

Obliteration through violent assault is multi-dimensional in "Where Are You Going." The domestic space, a house as the nurturing place of childhood, yields to attack from outside no less than the body, consciousness, even "heart" of the girl is forced to give way. Observing that the house looks solid, Friend tells Connie, "Now, put your hand on your heart, honey. . . . That feels solid too but we know better." And when Connie feels her own pounding heart, "she thought for the first time in her life that it was nothing that was hers, that belonged to her." If "Where Are You Going" is the story of the end of childhood, the end of romance, the invasion and probable destruction of private and self-contained space provide one important definition of private and self-contained space provide one important definition of the end of innocence. Friend's taking over the "heart" of the young girl so that "it was nothing that was hers" spells a conquest of both space and will: his intimation that he will wait for and then kill the family if Connie does not go with him is the more terrible because of Connie's own ambivalent feelings about her family, the breaking in the child's trust in her parents. Finally, the satanic visitor's incantation, "We'll go out to a nice field, out in the country where it smells nice and it's sunny," represents not only a chilling perversion of pastoral—for the words of Satan can lead not toward, but only away from, Eden—but a ritualized statement that all of the walls defining an individual self have been destroyed. Connie's pushing open the screen door to go off with Arnold Friend, the ultimate yielding, signifies that indeed the place she came from "ain't there any more."

☐ *Notes* ■

1. Susan Brownmiller, *Against Our Will* (New York: Simon and Schuster, 1975), p. 14.
2. Mario Praz, *Conversation Pieces: A Survey of the Informal Group Portrait in Europe and America* (University Park, Pa.: Penn-

sylvania State University Press, 1971), 68–70. Praz discusses Hogarth in particular, noting the latter's interest in viewing his family groups as characters in a drama. For an analysis of the image of the chaste maiden in eighteenth-century fiction, see Marlene LeGates, "The Cult of Womanhood in Eighteenth-Century Thought," *Eighteenth Century Studies* 10 (Fall 1976), 21–39. The motif of seduction in the literature of sentiment is treated particularly in R. F. Brissenden, *Virtue in Distress* (New York: Barnes and Noble, 1974).

3. Lawrence Stone has explored privacy as an aspect of the "closed domesticated nuclear family" in *The Family, Sex, and Marriage in England 1500–1800* (New York: Harper and Row, 1977), p. 253. The subject has been provocatively treated in Richard Sennett, *The Fall of Public Man* (New York: Knopf, 1977), but Sennett does not fully appreciate the tension between private and public in sentimental literature.

B. RUBY RICH ■

Good Girls, Bad Girls

There is a wonderful movie called *Smooth Talk*. It ends when its teenage protagonist, Connie, has a fight with her mom and stays home alone. There is a horrible movie called *Smooth Talk*. It starts when a psychopath in a gold convertible comes looking for Connie, alone in an empty house.

If you want to see one of this season's finest films, walk out of the 68th Street Playhouse when Connie's family drives off to their barbecue. If you want to see one of the most pernicious pieces of moralism to emerge from a woman director in the 1980s, then stick around.

Smooth Talk is Joyce Chopra's critically acclaimed new movie, but, its boosters to the contrary, this film offers neither the screen's most delectable seduction nor the definitive female coming-of-age portrait. No, what Chopra offers, with the help of the predictably nasty Joyce Carol Oates story that is her springboard, is a punishment to fit the crime of sexual desire. *Smooth Talk* may be the first genuinely postfeminist movie, unless it's just a belated prefeminist one.

The first half of *Smooth Talk,* is indeed an engaging and finely observant study of adolescent female sexuality and narcissism, relations between a family and its pubescent girl-child, and, most astonishingly, the combination of fear and desire (what used to be called "thrill") of virginal sex. It provides the grand drama of going, not All the Way, but at least a ways down the road. We see Connie rehearsing come-on lines in front of her mirror, cruising the mall boys with her girlfriends only to dissolve into giggles if any come close, and infuriating

---

From the *Village Voice* (April 15, 1986): 69.

her mom and stay-at-home sister with the omni-presence of her newfound sexuality. Her make-out scenes, in the parked cars of a succession of teenage boys, are so hot they'll define the genre.

But watch out. This movie is made by a moralist. For pleasure like that, Connie—and the audience—must pay.

The second half of *Smooth Talk* is a nightmare. The film drags two red herrings across our path, scary moments in a deserted parking garage and a dark road abuzz with over-amplified crickets and a car of drunken boys. But these are mere plot embroidery. It is broad daylight when Connie's family heads out with the charcoal and Arnold Friend pulls up in his golden chariot, intent on having his way with Connie, and mesmerizes her into rape by verbal coercion. In this half of the movie, Chopra uses the whole bag of cinematic tricks. Every time Connie is on screen, she's shot in close-up, tightly, claustrophobically, with no space around her, pinned into that tiny unmovable frame. Every time Arnold is on-screen, he's in middle shot, framed against an ample landscape, lots of space around him, master of the territory. The music surges on the soundtrack. It isn't long before the high-spirited Connie is a quivering puddle on the hallway floor.

What has happened here? *Smooth Talk* softens up its audience with lust and flirtation, then slices through its gut with a knife of horror. It turns into a familiar product, the stock in trade of the horror genre: woman alone, trapped in empty house, terrorized, raped or killed or left insane. In Chopra's hands, the knife has a twist: Connie is punished for sex with sex. Connie is singled out for rape because she's guilty of being pretty and flirtatious. She was asking for it, wasn't she? Just looking for it, right? We're back in the familiar terrain of Blame the Victim Land.

Smooth Talk is an insidious movie, and a curious one. Thirteen years ago, Joyce Chopra made a name for herself as a feminist documentary filmmaker with *Joyce at 34*, a self-portrait of her pregnancy. Now, she's the 48-year-old mother of a teenage daughter. And she's made a movie with a message for teenage daughters everywhere: keep a lid on your sexuality, don't you dare express it, don't you ever act out those "trashy daydreams" (as Connie's mother puts it), or you'll get

142

it. Like a grownup bogeyman, Arnold Friend will come and get you. *Smooth Talk* is a movie that means to teach teenage girls the perils of sex. Worst of all, the film carries out its mission with a massively mixed message. Connie is terrorized with words, reduced to dumb paralysis, abducted from her home, returned to her doorstep after an offscreen rape . . . and this is praised by some critics as a masterful cinematic "seduction." Joyce Chopra is praised as a major new talent. But a talent in the service of what? The phenomenon of a feminist filmmaker from the 1970s emerging in the middle of this decade to put young women in their place does not, for me, go down easy.

Even more disturbing than the critical raves and festival accolades was the reaction of 68th Street Playhouse's posh audience: overwhelmingly middle-aged, they laughed all through the first half and then kept on laughing right through Connie's disintegration. I suspect the lure of *Smooth Talk* is a simple one: the spectacle of lust delivered into the audience, and then the punishment of its female embodiment, again for audience pleasure. If people tell you they like this film, be skeptical. Ask who *they* were in high school: the desexualized Good Girl? the nerd that so many Connies rejected? *Smooth Talk* provides vicarious retribution for a wide audience. Meanwhile, if you know any teenage girls, keep them away from this movie just on the off chance that the antiporn crowd might be right and that movies really can affect behavior. *Smooth Talk* is an old-fashioned mother's dream: fleeing the consequences of her sexuality, Connie returns to the bosom of her family, to the literalization of mamma's arms. That's what Joyce Chopra might call a happy ending.

☐ BRENDA O. DALY ■

An Unfilmable Conclusion: Joyce Carol Oates at the Movies

In 1966, three years before the shocking stories of Charles Manson and his "family" emerged, *Life* magazine carried the story of a murderer named Charles Schmid.[1] With the help of teenage "followers," Schmid murdered three young women and buried them in the desert outside Tucson. "The Pied Piper of Tucson" was later exposed by a side-kick, tried, and sent to prison. Locking Schmid up did not, of course, make America a less violent or safer place to live. It was to explore this "senseless" violence in terms of its cultural implications that Joyce Carol Oates wrote her well-known short story, "Where Are You Going, Where Have You Been?" first published in the fall of 1966. In the story Charles Schmid, renamed "Arnold Friend," retains his too-large cowboy boots and pancake make-up, as well as his "Golden Car" and his habit of using "high falutin' language." But Oates transforms him into a friend/fiend— a harbinger of "Death"—whose significance has since been widely discussed in introductory literature classes in colleges and universities.

Twenty years after its first appearance, this widely anthologized story has been made into a movie called "Smooth Talk," released in 1986. Directed by Joyce Chopra, it stars Laura Dern as "Connie," Treat Williams as "Arnold Friend," and Mary Kay Place as Connie's mother. This intense inter-

From the *Journal of Popular Culture* 23 (Winter 1989): 101–114.

est—evident in the translations from fact, into fiction and film—raises a number of questions: Why, for example, has yet another woman artist resurrected a tale of violence against women? Whose story is being told, and what are its larger cultural implications? Any response to these questions requires analysis of the relationship among many different texts: popular music, magazines, and books (some of which Schmid drew upon to create his persona), as well as medieval art, nineteenth-century American literature, and critical essays on Yeats.

One problem that Oates and Chopra emphasize—the psychosocial implications of space—is not a new preoccupation of women artists. For example, Sandra Gilbert and Susan Gubar argue in *The Madwoman in the Attic* that "anxieties about space seem to dominate the literature of the nineteenth century by women and their twentieth-century descendents.[2] For women writers this anxiety about space is not simply metaphysical, but social, according to Gilbert and Gubar. The fact that most agoraphobics are women supports this argument, as does the fact the male readers tend to resist the gothic whose claustrophobic spaces have long identified this genre as for women readers.[3] The gothic spaces of works such as *Jane Eyre* and "The Yellow Wallpaper" further illustrate Gilbert and Gubar's point, and in "Where Are You Going, Where Have You Been?" it is easy to recognize Oates as a twentieth-century descendent. Oates is, in fact, frequently described as a "gothic" writer although this term, sometimes used pejoratively, is too limited. Spatial inequalities are apparent even in Oates's title, "Where Are You Going, Where Have You Been?" Such questions are often put to teenagers by parents, many of whom grant greater freedom of movement to boys. Probably one reason that parents continue to constrain their daughters is that it is still possible for a girl—out late at night and in public places—to be put on trial and found guilty of her own rape/murder.[4] At one level, then, both Oates and Chopra are examining a woman's lack of freedom, and her vulnerability to male violence, in our culture. Indeed, "spatial limitations are of crucial concern" in Oates's story, as Christina Marsden Gillis has pointed out, and the "invasion of personal, interior space" occurs at many levels.[5] I see similar concern with spatial limitations and invasions of personal space in Chopra's film.

Both women use space to signify Connie's lack of sexual and social equality, but what is lost in the translation from fiction to film can only be understood by moving beyond the realistic plane of interpretation to allegory. In a review of Chopra's film, Oates explains that her allegorical intentions were perhaps "too explicit" in an earlier title, "Death and the Maiden."[6] Despite the loss of this title, borrowed from a fifteenth-century German engraving by Albrecht Dürer, critics have noted Friend's Satanic appearance and Connie's role as "Everyman."[7] In addition, as I will illustrate, Oates's allusions to Dickinson, especially "Because I Could Not Stop for Death," suggest that the story may be read as allegory. Finally, it is perhaps in the lyrics of Bob Dylan's "It's All Over Now, Baby Blue"—and Oates has dedicated the story to Dylan— that the historical and political implications of "Where Are You Going, Where Have You Been?" can best be understood. At this level of meaning the question of the title, addressed to readers, asks us to consider how an act of violence— apparently without motive—can teach us something about our culture. Oates's tale of rape may also be compared to Yeats's "Leda and the Swan," an allegory of power and knowledge that had preoccupied Oates in the 1960s in both her fiction—*A Garden of Earthly Delights* (1966)—and in critical essays on Yeats.[8] Although these allegorical allusions are, understandably, lost in the film, Oates nevertheless credits Chopra with "an accomplished and sophisticated film" and, noting the change in her story's ending, describes her own ambiguous conclusion as "unfilmable." The loss is significant since, at this moment in Oates's story, Connie sees beyond Arnold Friend's limited, though powerful, vision.

Yet "Smooth Talk" certainly deserves praise, particularly its fidelity to Oates's spatial analogies. Nevertheless, one film critic has complained that Oates's "predictably nasty" story has, in Chopra's medium, become a formulaic cautionary tale for girls. Largely through its spatial vocabulary, B. Ruby Rich argues in "Good Girls, Bad Girls," the film warns girls to stay home and "keep a lid on their sexuality."[9] Chopra uses "the whole bag of cinematic tricks," complains Rich, to enforce a sexual/spatial system of inequalities:

> Every time Connie is on screen, she's shot in close-up, tightly, claustrophobically, with no space around her, pinned into the tiny unmoveable frame. Every time Arnold is on screen, he's in middle-shot framed against an ample landscape, lots of space around him, master of the territory. The music surges on the soundtrack. It isn't long before the high-spirited Connie is a quivering puddle on the hallway floor.

Rich exaggerates only slightly. In fact, at moments we do see Connie in a wider frame—at the beach or the shopping center, for example—but it is also true that each time Connie moves into public spaces, traditionally "male" territory, danger lurks in the form of a shadowy male who, as the movie progresses, becomes increasingly more threatening. And each time Connie crosses over into new and larger spaces—such as the moment when Connie crosses the highway to the drive-in—she becomes increasingly more vulnerable. Also, at each crossing she becomes more isolated as, one by one, her girl friends drop out of the adventure, usually under orders from a parent.

The "high-spirited" Connie is indeed trapped by the rapist in an isolated house where she has been left alone by her parents and sister. Yet, just as Oates and Chopra did not invent the spatial inequalities they depict, they also do not simply repeat a horror formula which, at a woman's expense, will titillate an audience. Rich claims that when Friend arrives at Connie's doorstep the film "turns into a familiar product, the stock in trade of the horror genre: woman alone, trapped in empty house, terrorized, raped or killed or left insane." The innovative dialogue that Oates locates at this threshold— much of which Chopra employs in the film—is certainly not formulaic, nor is the conclusion of either the film or the story, as I shall demonstrate. Furthermore, when Rich says that the appeal of the formula, supposedly merely repeated by Oates and Chopra, is "the spectacle of lust delivered unto the audience, and then punishment of its embodiment, again for audience pleasure," she forgets that in the film Connie survives and in fiction, though not likely to survive, Connie "awakens" spiritually and, thus, sees beyond F(r)iend. What she sees, "the vast sunlit reaches of the land behind him and on all sides of him," is "alive." Oates says in her preface, "What seemed to be dead—the world-matter surrounding us—has been discovered to be living, intensely alive."[10] Connie may be moving toward a kind of death—toward her final "home"—but she understands, as Oates says in her Preface, that "What seemed to be dead—the concept of 'God'—is waking up, returning to consciousness." Connie's grave, her "Cornice—in the Ground," is the site of her new home, her new life.[11] In a profound sense, then, Oates's Connie is as "high-spirited" as Chopra's assertive survivor. Oates makes this comment about the film's ending: "Laura Dern's Connie is no longer 'my' Connie at the film's conclusion; she is very much alive, assertive, strong-willed—a girl, perhaps, of the mid-1980s and not of the mid-1960s."

The evolution of Connie's consciousness—as she faces death—is the focus of Oates's story. Schmid was the central figure in *Life,* but in successive drafts of the tale, Oates shifted Friend to the margins as Connie's consciousness became central. Chopra's title, "Smooth Talk," gives star billing to Friend, but Connie has the last, assertive word. Neither artist blames the victim; instead they tell her story, breaking the silence imposed upon rape victims. Connie's story is one of joy in her awakening sexuality, a "goodness" that challenges the convention of virginal goodness. It is Connie's mother, whose morality is conventional, who forces Connie to disguise her sexuality. Thus Connie has "two sides" that "looked one way when she was at home and another way when she was away from home. Everything had two sides to it." Yet in her Preface Oates explains that neither side is "evil" according to her moral vision:

> A new morality is emerging in America which may appear to be opposed to the old but which is in fact a higher form of the old—the democratization of the spirit, the experiencing of life as meaningful in itself, without divisions into 'good' and 'bad,' 'beautiful' or 'ugly,' 'moral' or 'immoral.'

Younger readers seem to understand this evolution in consciousness, says Oates, and Chopra shares this vision. Chopra
has invented some wonderfully amusing scenes that illustrate
her pleasure in Connie's "trying on" of her new sexuality:
Connie practicing boy/girl dialogue before her bathroom mirror; Connie changing her clothes in the shopping center bathroom; or Connie trying on a revealing outfit to wear to the
drive-in. She's lovely.

The film audience is certainly not meant to share the
attitude of Connie's mother who describes the "good" June
and the "bad" Connie on the phone, who rejects Connie when
she tries to join the family at playing cards, and who expects
Connie to fulfill her own emotional emptiness. The mother's
sexual jealousy is obvious. One scene, especially, shows the
limits of her older morality: when Connie's mother asks about
"the Pettinger girl," Connie confronts her mother with her
own premarital sexuality. In return for this remark, Connie
is slapped. Despite her motherly love for Connie, she cannot
express a more genuine concern—that Connie's early sexual
maturity may trap her into a loveless marriage—because she
thinks judgmentally, in terms of the old morality. A failure of
imagination is evident in other family relationships as well.
The father—invented by Chopra—cannot seem to "imagine"
what his wife does all day. Their lives are gendered, their
imaginations limited by a kind of "innocence," a narrow vision
of the American dream, bounded by the material world. They
cannot move into one another's minds—past boundaries of
gender and generation—and this failure of imagination has
harsh consequences for Connie. For example, when Connie
lies to her father, telling him her mother knows of her crossing
the highway to the drive-in, he doesn't check her story, probably because he talks rarely with his wife. Such divisions
among the family—including those between the two sisters—
leads to Connie's isolation in the house on the day of Friend's
visit.

Arnold Friend will challenge the very limits of Connie's
consciousness. At the doorway, the threshold of Connie's body/
consciousness, Oates intensifies the crisis. As Christina Marsden Gillis interprets the story:

The seduction motif functions successfully in "Where are you going?" because the delineation of interior space figured in the female body analogizes invasion at several levels; the domestic space, the state of childhood consciousness associated with the home, and, of course, the individual consciousness.

The house-body equation operates on yet another level in both fiction and film: house-culture. It is not, finally, Connie's house, but her father's. As Friend warns, "'Your Daddy's house is nothing but a cardboard box I can knock down anytime.'" Connie's quick submission to Friend reveals her attitude toward masculine authority. Invited to take a ride, Connie asks, "'Where?'"—to which Friend responds, "'Where what?'" When she answers as if already under his command, "'Where are we going?'" Friend's psychic invasion has begun.

The question, "Where are we going?" takes on more sinister connotations as Oates's allegorical intentions become evident. To compensate for this loss of allusive language, Chopra relies on camera work to heighten oppositions: inside/outside, masculine/feminine, good/evil. Like her shadow, Friend mocks Connie's movements as she retreats when invited to look at "the other side" of his car. Connie also sees herself reflected in Friend's dark glasses, and both listen to the same music playing inside and outside the house. The sound-track suddenly becomes sinister, however, as Connie begins to suspect that Friend is not what he pretends to be: an ordinary teenager dressed in blue jeans and cowboy boots. At least some of Friend's strangeness is lost when Chopra omits his makeup and wobbly boots. Oates had employed these details, based on the *Life* magazine article, to develop her allegory, suggesting the fiend's cloven hooves when she describes the rapist standing with "one of his boots . . . at a strange angle, as if the foot wasn't in it." Given Chopra's realistic mode, these details would have seemed too bizarre—despite their origin in fact—but the camera accentuates Friend's potential for violence, as well as his role as a double. In the shadows outside the house, Friend's face looms at the window; then his body darkens in the doorway. Friend speaks softly, as if romantically, with Connie, but he yells in harsh, angry tones at his "other" side, Ellie

Oscar, whose name suggests the fiend's "feminine" aspects. Then Ellie acts out his role as side-kick, or double, by ransacking Connie's bedroom while, off-screen, Friend violates Connie's body.

Chopra does retain the rapist's "civility," his manner of invading Connie's romantic daydreams before claiming her body. "'I ain't late am I?'" he asks, immediately defining the encounter. When Connie protests that she doesn't know him, he demonstrates his rhetorical skills and possible psychic power by knowing her music, her friends, her family, and even her private thoughts. He appears as unhurried as Dickinson's "civil" gentleman caller, who "knew no haste," but this very mixture of civility and threat creates the ambiguity—and terror—for his victim. When Friend says, "'Connie, this is your day set aside for a ride with me, and you know it,'" she first thinks this man might fulfill her "the way it was in movies and promised in songs." Yet the sudden strangeness of the man—his face appears much older and his romantic promises become threats—leads Connie to feel estranged from the material world—her house, her body—and increasingly aware of an invisible realm of which Friend is the emissary. The recognition is violent: forced to imagine her own rape/murder, Connie becomes detached from her own breathing, her own cries:

> She felt her breath jerking back and forth in her lungs as if it were something Arnold Friend was stabbing her with again and again with no tenderness. A noisy sorrowful wailing rose about her and she was locked inside it the way she was locked inside this house.

Connie calls out to her mother, but finally hangs up the phone, obeying Friend so that he will keep his promise not to "come inside" the house. At the same time Friend also promises to "come inside . . . where it's all secret."

Yet in both fiction and film perhaps Friend's most persuasive moment occurs when he implicates Connie in imagining her absent family. Like an artist, he sketches in just enough detail so that Connie, along with readers, begins to fill in missing details. Gazing into the distance, as a storyteller does, Friend creates this scene:

> "Right now they're—uh—drinking. Sitting around," he said vaguely, squinting as if he were staring all the way to town and over Aunt Tillie's backyard. Then the vision seemed to get clear and he nodded energetically, "Yeah, sitting around. There's your sister in a blue dress, huh? and high heels, the poor sad bitch—nothing like you sweetheart! And your mother's helping some fat woman with the corn, they're cleaning the corn—husking the corn—"
> "What fat woman?" Connie cried.

And he's got her. She's trapped by his language, mastered by his vision. However, in their different texts both Chopra and Oates "steal the language" from Friend, redefining the encounter, revising Connie's "end." Oates's ambiguous conclusion does not reflect one of the greatest social changes in the past decade: the feminist movement. Had Connie lived in the 1980s she might have been a "resisting reader"—a girl less vulnerable to lines from movies and lyrics from popular songs, a girl who insists upon defining reality in her *own* language. Let me now turn to the different visions of Connie's end, first in the film, then in fiction.

Chopra's "Golden Car" doesn't turn into what Oates calls "Death's Chariot (a funky souped-up convertible)." However, when Connie returns from her ride, after being raped by Friend, the car has certainly lost its glitter, its glamour. Chopra does criticize the consumerism that disguises a greater American dream by emphasizing, as Oates does, the cars, houses, and hamburgers that define the desires of her characters. Shopping centers and drive-ins are, for Connie and her friends, like places of worship. In a comic addition to the story, Chopra has Connie's father share with her, not his wife, his pleasure and satisfaction in owning a piece of property and sitting outside in his lawn chair whenever he wants. If he has any other desire—such as painting his house, as his wife wishes—viewers don't hear it. Little wonder, then, that Connie's awakening sexuality is shaped by the values expressed by popular music, advertising, and movies. Chopra also suggests with her camera what Oates describes in Arnold's sinister behavior—his "sniffing" at Connie as if "she were a treat he was going to gobble up"—that Connie herself may be perceived as a consumer object. Connie clearly rejects Friend's vision when, at the end of the film, she warns him not to return. Furthermore, when Connie dances with her sister June—in space Ellie Oscar has ransacked—she gains back some territory. Significantly, the music is the same that Connie and her mother had danced to earlier, though in separate rooms. In the end, then, Connie and her family are "musically" reunited, though Connie understands that she cannot tell her "innocent" family her story: that she has been raped. What Connie realizes is that, given her family's view of morality, she will be regarded as a "bad girl," as somehow to blame for the violence she has suffered.

It is precisely this morality that Oates believes we must move beyond. The ambiguous conclusion of "Where Are You Going, Where Have You Been?" prompts readers to analyze the question posed by the title and to move beyond the more obvious answers—those that remain within the realm of the visible world—just as the rhetoric of Arnold Friend forces Connie to move beyond the borders of her father's house. Connie knows, for example, that when Friend calls her "my sweet little blue-eyed girl" it "had nothing to do with her brown eyes." Chopra's Connie knows this too, at least on the level of the rapist's psychological attitude toward women: they're all the same to him, for only his masculinity counts. Oates carries this psychological complexity even further, linking the rapist's "little blue-eyed girl" to the "vast sunlit reaches of the land." Readers who know Dylan's "It's All Over Now, Baby Blue" may interpret this vague phrase as reference to Connie's death: Connie will soon be buried in the ground. The film, of course, cannot develop this allusion, except through its soundtrack, but once again, death isn't consistent with Chopra's revised ending. Yet, in framing the movie—which begins at the beach, moves for its climax (his/not hers) to the mountains, then returns to Connie's home—Chopra does suggest a power greater than the so-called civilized world. What had seemed a mere backdrop for human activity does "come alive" for Connie, even in the film.

Oates's story suggests that this consciousness of the "vast sunlit land" is repressed—like evil—by our civilized minds. But the unconscious threat of the earth, to which we must one day return, shapes our desire for a sense of belonging. Both the victim and the victimizer share this desire to be part of something larger, a family, a community, a country. Their shared music hints at this, as does their shared vision of the picnicing family. Chopra emphasizes this similarity through parallel scenes, both of which show Connie and Friend as "outsiders." Just as Arnold had stood alone in the darkness outside the drive-in, Connie stands alone in the darkness outside her home as her family plays cards. Significantly, Connie's isolation from her family increases as her sexuality becomes stronger, as if her father's house cannot contain, cannot allow, this erotic disturbance, and therefore relegates a woman's sexuality to the "outside," defining it as "evil." Yet both Oates and Chopra move beyond this binary morality— and beyond the formulaic horror show—in their endings. When Connie asserts herself in the film, she moves beyond her rapist, but her victory—unlike his conquest of her—does not violate him. No simple reversal of roles occurs. Oates achieves a victory for Connie by implying that she chooses to sacrifice herself to protect her family from Friend. Despite her impending death, strongly foreshadowed in Oates's dialogue, one way to interpret the story is that Connie acts heroically.

Oates articulates Connie's "higher consciousness" through allusions to Dylan's music and Dickinson's poetry. Dickinson's carriage becomes the vehicle by which one imagines what Connie "sees" behind and on all sides of the f(r)iend. In "Because I could not stop for Death," Death seems to be in the driver's seat, like Friend. But Dickinson's carriage also has a passenger named "Immortality." This immortality becomes visible when the poem raises the question of what moves, what sees:

> We passed the School, where Children strove
> At recess—in the Ring—
> We passed the Fields of Gazing Grain—
> We passed the Setting Sun—

And, in the next line, "Or rather—He passed Us." Now the speaker's point of view, and consciousness, seem to have altered: if Grain is "Gazing," it must be alive. If what "passed" is not the carriage, but the "Setting Sun" then it, too, is alive. From this larger perspective, humankind appears circumscribed, like "recess—in the Ring," like the striving of "Children." Dylan makes a similar point in "It's All Over Now, Baby Blue." The lyrics describe a world alive, a world in motion: "The carpet too, is moving under you / And it's all over now, baby blue." This living world includes: "the sky too, is folding under you / And it's all over now, baby blue." If one's identity seems certain, Dylan questions even this, in lyrics eerily suggestive of Arnold Friend at Connie's door: "the vagabond who's rapping at your door / Is standing in the clothes that you once wore."[12] Nothing stays, nothing is solid, not Connie's house, not even her heart: "That feels solid too but we know better," Friend tells her.

Like Death—Dickinson's unhurried gentleman caller—Friend easily destroys mere things—houses, cars, bodies. What Dickinson implies, however, is that Death hasn't the power to destroy the invisible realm. In this realm, a grave becomes a new house:

> We paused before a House that seemed
> A swelling in the Ground
> The roof was scarcely visible—
> The Cornice—in the Ground—

To compare a grave to a house is to suggest that one "lives" in a grave. Like Oates, then, Dickinson implies that the earth itself is "alive," a form of life that, though it may absorb individual identities and human consciousness, nevertheless lives. And the "voice" of Dickinson's poem does achieve a kind of Immortality, just as the voice of Connie and her assailant become Immortal through the creative consciousness of Oates and Chopra. Of course, audiences must animate these artistic creations and, thus, this consciousness is never simply individual. Connie mistakenly assumes that her lovers will affirm her individual fantasies, her vision of herself. Friend disabuses her of that faulty notion. However, by destroying her romantic

156

fantasies, Friend awakens in her a consciousness of powers greater than the self—family, community and "the vast sunlit land."

In Annette Kolodny's historical analysis of "the-land-as-woman," she shows how this imaginative gendering of the land served the American need to deny the threat of the unknown. Kolodny asks, "Was there perhaps a *need* to experience the land as a nurturing, maternal breast because of the threatening, alien, and potentially emasculating terror of the unknown?"[13] In an unsettled land such terrors would be greater and, perhaps for this reason, European pastorals— "Eden, Paradise, the Golden Age, and the idyllic garden"— were transformed into "an American promising material ease," as if this dream were "a daily reality," says Kolodny. Connie and her family represent this American mythologizing of daily reality—of which the shopping center becomes a symbol— and Arnold represents the dark side of this dream of the land of plenty: the necessity to conquer the land, to master it, to take from it without giving anything back. This evil is cultural, as Tom Quirk writes in his analysis of the source of Oates's story. He asks, "Isn't Tucson—out there in the Golden West, in the grand setting where the skies are not cloudy all day— supposed to be a flowering of the American dream?" He describes Oates's story as a "withering reply," as "very nearly a suspenseful parody of the West and Home on the Range."[14] As Quirk says, the graves of three young women—ages thirteen, fifteen, and seventeen—in the desert outside Tucson give this dream a sinister twist.

The sunny and sinister are also illustrated by the community that spawned Charles Schmid. According to the *Life* magazine article, the Tucson community consisted of a disproportionate number of elderly people, drawn there by the promise of sun and warmth in their retirement. Schmid's generous monthly income of $300 came from his parents who ran a nursing home, but Schmitty's teenage accomplices came from those less financially privileged, those who didn't "belong." Later, Charles Manson also created his "family" from those children who in some way didn't belong. The dream of belonging, translated primarily into economic terms, disenfranchises many, creating the rage and hunger that Schmid and Manson could manipulate. To satisfy their spiritual hunger, Schmid and Manson accumulated girls who became their property. Schmid, who read *Playboy* and a Jules Feiffer novel called *Harry, the Rat with Women,* had declared it "his ambition to be like Harry and have a girl commit suicide over him." Like Schmid, though on a grander scale, Manson would achieve significance and power—both denied him by an indifferent society—through violence.[15] These criminals, though seemingly *outside* ourselves, nevertheless act as messengers of the spiritual world constantly being denied by narrowly materialist visions of the land of plenty. As Oates says in her preface:

> There are cultures in which divinity is spread out equally, energizing everyone and everything; there are other cultures—unfortunately ours is one of them—in which the concept of "divinity" was snatched up by a political/economic order, and the democratic essence of divinity denied.

As Oates interprets the violence of a Charles Schmid, then, his acts, paradoxically, affirm a higher consciousness: the democratic essence of divinity. For this greater reality, a spiritual reality, the material world is a text to be read as the medievalists interpreted their world. At the same time, Oates's insistence upon the democracy of the spirit challenges medieval hierarchies, and thus, her story, "Death and the Maiden," is radically revisionary. By emphasizing the relationship between past and present artists, however, Oates illustrates that her "new morality" is not "opposed to the old but . . . a higher form of the old." Within the context of this new morality, Connie's death is not an "end," but the sign of a cultural change. As Connie moves across the threshold of her old house to her new house in the "sunlit land," she thus becomes a harbinger of a new consciousness.

What is this new consciousness? In her essays on Yeats, both written in the late 1960s, Oates describes it as "the tragic fact of metamorphosis . . . at the heart of Yeats's poetry,"[16] a belief also at the heart of Oates's fiction during this period. For example, in her novel *A Garden of Earthly Delights,* also published in 1966, Oates dramatizes the narrowing

158

of the American dream that has been "snatched up by a political economic order." A child named Swan who is conceived in love—and who initially has a sense of his kinship to the land—is destroyed by economic realities. His mother Clara, born to migrant workers during the Great Depression, is abandoned by her lover during her pregnancy and this betrayal leads her, out of necessity, to abandon the dream of spiritual equality. Instead, the beautiful, pregnant Clara marries a wealthy farmer named "Revere," a man that her son Swan later kills before killing himself. What Oates illustrates through the characterization of both Clara and Connie is their reverence for false gods, their betrayal by hierarchies of class and gender. This same materialism also insists upon a view of the self as isolated and competitive, whereas Oates—again in her essay on Yeats—views the human personality as fluid. She says of Yeats's poetry:

> Half consciously he seems to have chosen this primitive "logical thought" over the more commonplace and sanitary belief in the permanent isolation of human beings from one another and from the world of nature, whether animals, plants, or inanimate matter. The primitive imagination accepts totally the fact of miraculous change: what would be miraculous to them is our conception of a conclusion, an ending of spirit and energy.

Oates's thought, I believe, is similarly "primitive," presenting Connie at the point of metamorphosis from one state of being to another, from one consciousness to another. By analogy, this moment of rape or violent metamorphosis, like the rape in Yeats's "Leda and the Swan," signals the violence of our cultural metamorphosis.

The difference between Oates's Connie and Chopra's Connie is but one instance of our cultural metamorphosis during the past 20–25 years. For such change, the conception of a conclusion—"an ending of spirit and energy"—would indeed seem "miraculous." In this sense, Oates's non-ending is certainly "unfilmable," for it portrays an energy—an erotic, spiritual energy signalled by violence—that cannot finally, be contained by a work of art. The conventions of realism especially—the insistence upon endings, and on "character" bounded by material realities including anatomical features—do not allow this higher consciousness to be invoked in Chopra's film. Oates has suggested its mystery by the use of a question in her title, "Where Are You Going, Where Have You Been?" and in the ambiguous conclusion of her story. She has also said, in a *Newsweek* interview in 1972, "I write about things that are violent and extreme, but it is always against a background of something deep and imperishable. I feel I can wade in blood," she said. "I can endure the 10,000 evil visions because there is this absolutely imperishable reality behind it."[17] Perhaps this imperishable reality is present not in a permanent "Connie," but in her metamorphosis through fiction, film and, of course, American life.

☐ *Notes* ∎

1. "The Pied Piper of Tucson," reprinted in this volume. In the mid-1970s Charles Schmid was stabbed to death by inmates at the Arizona State Penitentiary. No one was convicted of his murder, according to a corrections officer at the prison.

2. *The Madwoman in the Attic: The Woman Writer and the Nineteenth Century Literary Imagination* (New Haven: Yale University Press, 1979), p. 83.

3. "Gothic Possibilities" by Norman H. Holland and Leona F. Sherman in *Gender and Reading,* eds. Elizabeth A. Flynn and Patrocinio P. Schweickart (Baltimore: The Johns Hopkins Press, 1986). In their essay Holland and Sherman compare their gendered responses to the gothic. For example, Holland says, "For me, both identifying with a female and imagining being penetrated call into question my male identity" (p. 220). Sherman writes, "the gothic novel provides a polarizing of inside and outside with which an adult woman, particularly in a sexist society, might symbolize a common psychosocial experience; and invaded life within her mid, her body, her home, bounded by a social structure that marks off economic and political life as 'outside'" (p. 226).

4. The Donahue Show, 25 May 1988. Donahue's guest, Ellen Levin—mother of Jennifer Levin who was raped and killed by Robert Chambers in a New York city park—described how her daughter was

put on trial by the media and by the lawyers. Without proof, according to Levin, newspapers asserted that Jennifer's diary contained descriptions of "kinky sex." During the 1980s violent crimes against women, including rape, have been increasing.

    5. Gillis, "'Where Are You Going, Where Have You Been?': Seduction, Space and a Fictional Mode." Reprinted in this volume.

    6. "When Characters on the Page Are Made Flesh on the Screen," *The New York Times*, Sunday, 23 March 1986, p. 1, 22. All of Oates's comments about "Smooth Talk" are from this essay.

    7. Marie Mitchel Olesen Urbanski, "Existential Allegory": Joyce Carol Oates's "Where Are You Going, Where Have You Been?" Reprinted in this volume. I disagree with Urbanski's interpretation that Oates is telling the old story of "the seduction of Eve" in a contemporary setting. Oates is revising this story significantly. I also disagree that Connie's is a story of "*Everyman's* transition from the illusion of free will to the realization of externally determined fate." Connie does choose to walk through the door, however circumscribed this choice may seem. Other essays that examine the religious connotations of this story include Mark B. Robson's 'Joyce Carol Oates's "Where Are You Going, Where Have You Been?': Arnold Friend as Devil, Dylan, and Levite," in *Publications of the Mississippi Philological Association,* 1985, 98–105; Mike Tierce and John Michael Crafton's "Connie's Tambourine Man: A New Reading of Arnold Friend," *Studies in Short Fiction,* 1985 Spring, 22(2): 219–224, which interprets Friend as a Christ figure.

    8. "Yeats: Violence, Tragedy, Mutability" and "Tragic Rites in Yeats's *A Full Moon in March*," both in *The Edge of Impossibility: Tragic Forms in Literature* (New York: The Vanguard Press, 1972).

    9. "Good Girls, Bad Girls," *The Village Voice*, 15 April 1986. Reprinted in this volume. This review is, in part, a reply to an earlier review by Andrew Sarris called "Teenage Gothic," 4 March 1986. The controversy continued in a later edition (25 April 1986) when Sarris replied to Rich.

    10. "Preface" to *Where Are You Going, Where Have You Been? Stories of Young America* (Greenwich, Conn.: Fawcett, 1974).

    11. Sandra Gilbert and Susan Gubar, ed. *The Norton Anthology of Literature by Women: The Tradition in English* (New York: W. W. Norton, 1985), pp. 858–859. Buzzing flies in the story also suggest Dickinson's "I heard a Fly buzz—when I died."

    12. "Bob Dylan's Greatest Hits," Volume II, #7 on Compact

Disc, Columbia Records, 1971. "It's All Over Now, Baby Blue" was popular in the 1960s.

13. Annette Kolodny, *The Lay of the Land: Metaphor as Experience and History in American Life and Letters* (Chapel Hill: University of North Carolina Press, 1975), pp. 9 and 6.

14. Quirk, "A Source for 'Where Are You Going, Where Have You Been?'" Reprinted in this volume. Although I had discovered the *Life* magazine article prior to reading Quirk's essay, his emphasis on the American myth of the land has been suggestive.

15. In *The Triumph of the Spider Monkey* (New York: Fawcett Crest, 1976), Oates portrays a violent character called Bobbie Gotteson, and many of the details in this portrait bear a certain similarity to the Manson depicted in *Helter Skelter: The True Story of the Manson Murders* by Vincent Bugliosi with Curt Gentry (New York: W. W. Norton, 1974).

16. *Ibid.* "Tragic Rites in Yeats's *A Full Moon in March*," in *The Edge of Impossibility*, p. 169.

17. Walter Clemons, "Joyce Carol Oates: Love and Violence," *Newsweek* 11 December 1972, pp. 72–77.

❑ Selected Bibliography ∎

Works by Joyce Carol Oates

them (New York: Vanguard Press, 1968).
The Wheel of Love and Other Stories (New York: Vanguard Press, 1970).
Marriages and Infidelities (New York: Vanguard Press, 1972).
Bellefleur (New York: E. P. Dutton, 1980).
Angel of Light (New York: E. P. Dutton, 1981).
A Bloodsmoor Romance (New York: E. P. Dutton, 1982).
Solstice (New York: E. P. Dutton, 1985).
Marya: A Life (New York: E. P. Dutton, 1986).
You Must Remember This (New York: E. P. Dutton, 1987).
(Woman) Writer: Occasions and Opportunities (New York: E. P. Dutton, 1988).
American Appetites (New York: E. P. Dutton, 1989).
Because It Is Bitter and Because It Is My Heart (New York: E. P. Dutton, 1990).
Black Water (New York: E. P. Dutton, 1992).
Foxfire: Confessions of a Girl Gang (New York: E. P. Dutton, 1993).

Suggested Further Reading

Bender, Eileen Teper, *Joyce Carol Oates, Artist in Residence* (Bloomington: Indiana University Press, 1987).
Bloom, Harold, ed. *Modern Critical Views: Joyce Carol Oates* (New York: Chelsea House, 1987).
Creighton, Joanne V. *Joyce Carol Oates: Novels of the Middle Years* (New York: Twayne, 1992).
———. *Joyce Carol Oates* (Boston: Twayne, 1979).
Friedman, Ellen. *Joyce Carol Oates* (New York: Frederick Ungar, 1980).
Grant, Mary Kathryn. *The Tragic Vision of Joyce Carol Oates* (Durham: Duke University Press, 1978).
Johnson, Greg. *Understanding Joyce Carol Oates* (Columbia: University of South Carolina Press, 1987).
Milazzo, Lee, ed. *Conversations with Joyce Carol Oates* (Jackson: University Press of Mississippi, 1989).
Wagner, Linda, ed. *Critical Essays on Joyce Carol Oates* (Boston: G. K. Hall, 1979).

163

Waller, G. F. *Dreaming America: Obsession and Transgression in the Fiction of Joyce Carol Oates* (Baton Rouge: Louisiana State University Press, 1979).

Wesley, Marilyn C. *Refusal and Transgression in Joyce Carol Oates' Fiction* (Westport, Conn.: Greenwood Press, 1993).

❑ Permissions ■

Joyce Carol Oates, "Where Are You Going, Where Have You Been?" Copyright © 1991, The Ontario Review, Inc.

Don Moser, "The Pied Piper of Tucson," *Life,* March 4, 1966, 19–24, 80C–90.

Joyce Carol Oates, "'Where Are You Going, Where Have You Been?' and *Smooth Talk:* Short Story into Film," from *(Woman) Writer: Occasions and Opportunities.* Copyright © 1988 by The Ontario Review, Inc. Used by permission of the publisher, Dutton, an imprint of New American Library, a division of Penguin Books USA Inc.

Marie Mitchell Olesen Urbanski, "Existential Allegory: Joyce Carol Oates's 'Where Are You Going, Where Have You Been?'" *Studies in Short Fiction* 15 (1978): 200–203. Reprinted by permission of the publisher and Newberry College.

Tom Quirk, "A Source for 'Where Are You Going, Where Have You Been?'" *Studies in Short Fiction* 18 (1981): 413–420. Reprinted by permission of the publisher and Newberry College.

Joan D. Winslow, "The Stranger Within: Two Stories by Oates and Hawthorne," *Studies in Short Fiction* 17 (1980): 262–268. Reprinted by permission of the publisher and Newberry College.

Joyce M. Wegs, "'Don't You Know Who I Am?': The Grotesque in Oates's 'Where Are You Going, Where Have You Been?'" *Journal of Narrative Technique* 5 (1975): 66–72. Reprinted by permission of the publisher.

Larry Rubin, "Oates's 'Where Are You Going, Where Have You Been?'" *Explicator* 42 (1984): 57–59. Copyright © 1984 by Heldref Publications, 4000 Albemarle St., N.W., Washington, D.C. Reprinted by permission of the publisher and the Helen Dwight Reid Educational Foundation.

Gretchen Schulz and R.J.R. Rockwood, "In Fairyland, without a Map: Connie's Exploration Inward in Joyce Carol Oates's 'Where Are You Going, Where Have You Been?'" *literature and psychology* 30 (1980): 155–167. Reprinted by permission of the publisher.

Christina Marsden Gillis, "'Where Are You Going, Where Have You Been?': Seduction, Space, and a Fictional Mode," *Studies in Short Fiction* 18 (1981): 65–70. Reprinted by permission of the publisher and Newberry College.

B. Ruby Rich, "Good Girls, Bad Girls," *Village Voice* (April 15, 1986): 69. Reprinted by permission of the author and *The Village Voice.*

Brenda O. Daly, "An Unfilmable Conclusion: Joyce Carol Oates at the Movies," *Journal of Popular Culture* 23 (Winter 1989): 101–114. Reprinted by permission of the publisher.